W9-BRC-717

# THE
# MUSHIN WAY
## TO
# PEAK
# PERFORMANCE

# THE
# MUSHIN WAY
## TO
# PEAK
# PERFORMANCE

### THE PATH TO PRODUCTIVITY,
### BALANCE, AND
### SUCCESS

## MICHAEL VELTRI

WILEY

For Chiara Joy

# CONTENTS

# INTRODUCTION
# THE AIKIDO WAY

The soldier and martial artist Morihei Ueshiba was about to die.

Ueshiba was in Inner Mongolia on a mission of peace, traveling through a remote mountain pass when, suddenly, he and his party were ambushed. Their enemies—Chinese Nationalist soldiers and armed bandits—made a sudden attack, firing weapons as Ueshiba's party scattered, looking for cover in the bare mountains.

Surrounded, outnumbered, Ueshiba prepared himself for death. He drew on the reserves of mental strength he had built in years of martial arts practice, military service, and Buddhist studies. Despite the ambush, a strange calmness came over him. He later described the moment this way:

"I could not move from where I stood. So when the bullets came flying toward me, I simply twisted my body and moved my head . . . I could see pebbles of white light flashing just before the bullets. I avoided them by twisting and turning my body, and they barely missed me."[1]

Ueshiba had spent years training in the martial art of *aiki-jutsu*, a brutal self-defense system that evolved out of classical Japanese swordsmanship. For the samurai, life and death were determined on the battlefield in milliseconds, with razor-sharp swords. Aiki-jutsu was the samurai's last line of self-defense; if he lost his sword, he could still fight with his empty hands.

But, in the early twentieth century, after his experience in Inner Mongolia, Ueshiba took the martial tradition of aiki-jutsu and created *aikido* (pronounced "eye-key-doe"), also called the "art of peace," "meditation in motion," or "moving Zen." Over the years, he had come to realize that success in martial arts comes not only from physical discipline but also from a deep calmness similar to what he felt on the mountain pass. Of that moment when time stopped, he said:

"The calmer I became, the clearer my mind became. I could intuitively see the thoughts, including the violent intentions, of the other. The calm mind is like the quiet center of a spinning top; because of the calm center, the top is able to spin smoothly and rapidly. It almost seems to be standing still. This is the clarity of mind and body that I experienced."[2]

Out of life-or-death combat came a moment of clarity; out of the art of war came a discipline of peace. Because of this foundation, aikido training emphasizes developing the student's inner strength, indomitable spirit, and deep awareness—of self and others.

## THE MODERN BATTLEFIELD

While most of us today do not have to confront angry groups of armed bandits, we face our own type of combat in the workplace. Our world is rapidly changing, and decisions often have to be made against a background of incomplete information, ambiguity, and competing interests. It is harder and harder for most of us to see clearly through the thickets of conflicting information, to avoid distraction, to understand what the real goals are, and to discern how to achieve them.

Over the course of this book, you will learn how to filter out the noise in your life in order to create the kind of clarity that allowed master Ueshiba, often called "*O-Sensei*," to literally dodge bullets. Guided by the Japanese concept of *mushin* (pronounced "moo-sheen"), which literally means "no-mind" and can further be defined as "no-fear" or "no-distractions," you'll learn to clear your mind to find the certainty and confidence you need to make empowered decisions when the pace is fast, the stakes are high, and the outcome unclear. You will learn to develop and harness your powers of inner strength, indomitable spirit, and deep awareness—of self and others.

When it is time to do battle, in the conference room or in a tense meeting, or when you are making high-risk decisions, you will discover that aikido's principles can help you do the impossible: turn certain defeat into true victory. What's more, this book will demonstrate how every conflict, every challenge, is a chance to win a new supporter by seeking harmony and balance. This is what I mean by *The Mushin Way*: it's an approach to life that's grounded in the kind of harmony and mindfulness that clears the way for quick, decisive action.

## What Is Aikido?

The Japanese word *aikido* is made up of three kanji characters: *ai* (合), which means "meeting" or "harmony," and is also a homonym for the word "love"; *ki* (気), which means "energy"; and *dō* (道), which means "path" or "road." So aikido means "the path you follow in learning to harmonize your energy"—with your opponent's, or the world's.

The discipline of aikido can be challenging for people who are used to traditional Western models of study where the student moves in a linear fashion from concept to concept. In aikido—as in other Eastern disciplines such as Zen meditation, calligraphy, and the tea ceremony—instead of progressing linearly from Point A to Point B, students circle around the mysteries of the discipline, looking at them from all angles, striving to get closer to the calm center of the spinning top that is the mind. The test is always the same: the one-on-one combat that is a metaphor for the battle the student must do with his or her own mind and ego.

Success in aikido is about learning to absorb or blend with your opponent's energy, rather than trying to land the hardest blow. It can be a very humbling discipline to study, because strength alone will not get you very far. In fact, it is often harder for stronger students to learn proper technique, because they can muscle their way through bouts on strength alone—until they come up against someone stronger than they are.

Aikido teaches the student that meeting force with force will never work, that the minute you choose to attack, you have lost, because you have gone outside of harmony. But it is not about being passive; it is about putting aside your fear and your self-absorption and acting to protect both yourself and your opponent. In fact, aikido enlarges your worldview to include your opponent's. It is a lesson that businesspeople often spend a lifetime trying without success to learn. After all, if you are unable to see what your competition is seeing, you are eventually going to fail.

This book will show you how to succeed by acting in harmony with your own nature instead of fighting yourself, by leveraging the strength of everyone around you instead of trying to act alone, and by maintaining a sense of balance instead of trying to push your way through a problem with brute force.

Most of us do not face a hail of bullets most days, but we do confront challenges that feel impossible. We do not believe we have the strength to fight the battles before us. Too often, when we find ourselves at a crossroads, we hesitate. We want to hold off on making the right choice because we are afraid. In this book, I will show you how to gain the clarity to make the right choices, how making those choices is empowering, and how even the most unlikely battles can be won.

## MY PATH TO AIKIDO

I first stumbled onto the principles of aikido as a U.S. Marine stationed in California. But in order to understand why this discipline appealed to me so deeply and how I came to make aikido the center of my life, we have to go back further.

I was born in the small town of Erie, Pennsylvania. My parents are wonderful, supportive people, who always taught me that I could be or do anything. But they were happy living the small-town life. I always yearned for something different. And that "something different" came to be symbolized by Japan and the world of martial arts.

It's a little embarrassing to admit now, but I think it was the TV show *Kung Fu* that first sparked my interest in martial arts. Of course, the idea of a Hollywood show about a Shaolin monk starring a white guy is cringeworthy today—but as a little kid growing up in Pennsylvania, all I knew was that martial arts were supercool, and the idea of the honorable warrior embedded in the show really spoke to me.

I'm not embarrassed at all to say that I grew up dreaming of becoming an honorable warrior in my own way. I took karate lessons for years in part because of that dream. Then, at 17, I decided to enlist in the Marines. I was drawn to the idea of becoming part of an elite team of fighters who lived by a code and fought together as a team. Plus, I knew I wanted to see the world, and the Marines' major international base is located in Okinawa, Japan. Joining the Marines would be my ticket to the place I still imagined as the birthplace of the samurai. So, right after I graduated from high school, I was off to Marine Corps boot camp in South Carolina.

As crazy as this might sound, I loved boot camp. It was probably the least stressful time in my life. Of course I was exhausted when I fell into my bunk every night, but everything was decided for me. I knew where I had to be and what I had to do to succeed. I loved being part of the team, loved pushing myself as hard as I could, loved having a structure of support around me that guided my energy in one singular direction.

## First Encounters

After boot camp, I was deployed to a base in California, near San Diego. Suddenly I had some free time, and I decided to look for a martial arts school. That's when I stumbled upon aikido.

From the first moment I saw aikido being practiced, I was hooked. It's a beautiful art to watch. It's very fluid—there's no offensive striking or kicking like there is in karate or many other martial arts disciplines. Aikido is a grappling art, like wrestling, in which the practitioner uses throws, joint locks, and other submissions to control a bigger and stronger attacker. The movements are all based on leverage. Something of that elegance communicated itself to me immediately, and I knew this was something I wanted to pursue.

So while I lived in California I settled into a routine. As soon as my shift was over at 4:30 PM, I was gone. I'd hop on my motorcycle and drive up the coast to the dojo where I was starting to learn the beautiful discipline of aikido. I was 19 years old, and I was willing to work as hard as I had to in order to learn.

## JOURNEY TO JAPAN

After two years in California, I was deployed to the Marine base in Okinawa, Japan. I went looking for an aikido school on the island, and as it happened, there was only one. That school was run by the man who became my teacher, mentor, and lifelong friend, Professor Iwao Yamaguchi.

I was originally stationed on the island for just a year, but I extended my deployment through the end of my enlistment, in 1993. I advanced to become a first-degree black belt in aikido while I was stationed on Okinawa—and I also started to learn my way around Japanese culture.

Of course, I made plenty of mistakes. I remember I visited this beautiful Buddhist temple pretty early on in my time on Okinawa. I was studying Japanese at the time, but I wasn't very good at it yet. I thought I was asking this monk what the name of the temple was—but every time I asked, he kept pointing down the hallway toward the bathrooms. Was this some kind of mysterious Zen nonanswer? Nope. Turns out, what I was actually asking him was not what is the temple called, but "What is the name of your honorable toilet?" The Japanese word for "temple" and "toilet" are very similar, and I was using the wrong word! This very patient monk was just pointing out the bathroom to me, over and over.

By the time my service in the Marine Corps was finished, I had learned a lot about aikido and about Japanese culture. But I knew I had more to learn. I decided to stay on, and I found a little-known visa that would allow me to stay for another year to study the culture. So for a year I lived the life of a traditional martial arts apprentice, studying with my teacher, Professor Yamaguchi. I also studied the Japanese language and Zen meditation. By the end of that year, I was approaching fluency in Japanese, and I was a second-degree black belt in aikido.

After that, I finished my college degree, studying part time at the prestigious International Christian University in Tokyo. I stayed on in Japan after I graduated, spending a year researching *keiretsu*, the large Japanese corporate conglomerates that dominate Japan's business landscape. My professional experience in Japan culminated in working for many years at a large international consulting firm helping Western Fortune 500 companies succeed in the Japanese market.

Finally, in 1999, I moved back to the United States, began working in the corporate world, and teaching aikido on the side. And then, in 2003, everything changed.

## THE INTERRUPTION

Right after my thirty-fourth birthday, I was diagnosed with testicular cancer—and instantly I was plunged into this whole other world. I went in for surgery less than 48 hours after my first doctor's appointment. The surgery went well. And for a couple of months the news was good. Until it wasn't.

Three months after my surgery, I found out the cancer had spread to my lung and I was going to have to go through chemo—really aggressive chemotherapy, all day, five days a week. My body felt completely destroyed. And yet, even after all that, there was still a spot on my lung in my postchemo scans. So I went in for another surgery. The doctors removed part of my left lung.

Thankfully, I've been cancer free since that surgery. But as you can imagine, my life has never been the same. After fighting cancer, the idea of quitting my stable corporate job to open a full-time aikido academy didn't sound scary at all. After all, what was the worst that could happen? The school could fail. So what? It wouldn't kill me.

I became a full-time business owner in 2006. I built a very successful aikido martial arts academy. Gradually, as I developed my aikido practice and worked with students from all sorts of walks of life, I started to see how the principles of the discipline could help me—and others—become more successful in my business career. I developed a coaching and consulting practice, and these days I speak all over the world, sharing aikido wisdom with groups at conferences, Fortune 500 companies, and elite organizations such as the Central Intelligence Agency.

## How the Book Is Structured: Applying the Principles of Aikido

In this book, I'll introduce you to 10 key principles that underpin the discipline of aikido. Each chapter will explain one of these core principles and introduce a physical or mental exercise that you can do to start to understand the principle and immediately put it into practice. In addition, each chapter has a final practical exercise that you can use to help improve your business or personal life. Throughout each chapter, I'll also share simple tips that will help you streamline your work and personal lives to attain clarity and peak performance.

The principles discussed in the book are the foundation of the philosophy of the beautiful martial art of aikido. It may sound strange to talk about a philosophy behind a martial art—after all, most Western sports don't really come with a philosophy. Basketball, baseball, and football all have rules. But martial arts are different, and aikido in particular is a discipline that combines demanding physical regimens with a spiritual side grounded in concepts drawn from Zen Buddhism and other Eastern philosophies.

The 10 principles we'll discuss in this book are:

## Chapter 1. 平気 Heiki: *Equanimity*

*Heiki*, pronounced "hey-key," literally means "calm energy." The word is often found in Buddhist *sutras*, or chants. It's often translated as "equanimity." We'll begin with this principle because none of the other work we'll do is possible without finding this kind of calm energy. We'll talk about how essential calm energy is during a crisis—and in daily life—and we'll discuss strategies for maintaining your calm no matter what is happening around you.

## Chapter 2. 気 Ki: *Energy*

*Ki*, pronounced "key," is life force. It's the physical and mental energy that flows through you at every moment of your life, powering everything you do. In aikido, students learn not only to use their ki but also to channel it. Aikido teaches us not to rely on pure strength alone. Strength can be seductive—if you rely too heavily on it, you're not learning the techniques properly. You're not learning how to direct your energy through the right channels, and that means you're not being as effective as you could be. In this chapter, we'll talk about how to harness and direct your energies in order to accomplish your goals.

### *Chapter 3.* 結び *Musubi: Connection*

Literally, *musubi* (moo-sue-bee) means tying a knot. In aikido, the word is used to mean connection—a powerful connection that links you to your deepest self, to your opponent, and to the world around you. In business and in life, musubi can help you see the world through the eyes of a customer, a colleague, or a friend or loved one. In this chapter, we'll discuss strategies for building these kinds of connections in order to get the people around you to support your goals.

### *Chapter 4.* 念 *Nen: One-Point*

Physically, in martial arts, the word *nen* (rhymes with "ten") refers to a point two inches below your navel: your center of gravity. Metaphysically, nen is a sense of cosmic balance. Ultimately, most of us would say we value the same things: family, friends, meaningful work, giving back to our communities. The much harder question is finding, and holding on to, a way to balance all those competing priorities in a way that feels right to you. In this chapter, I will explain how to set and hold on to proper life priorities, in order to find the path that truly works for you.

### *Chapter 5.* 無心 *Mushin: No-Mind/No-Distractions/ No-Fear*

*Mushin* (moo-sheen) is one of the most important concepts in aikido, and one of the most difficult to grasp. At the moment when you enter into battle—when you most want to have your wits about you—you are asked to empty your mind. Your conscious mind must let go of your training, your preparation, your thoughts about the contest to come. It must become still water, calm and clear. In this chapter, we will discuss strategies, including a formal meditation practice, that will help you clear your mind in the midst of day-to-day distractions.

## Chapter 6. 入り身 Irimi: *To Enter*

Aikido requires practitioners to go against their own instincts when faced with a conflict. You have to move toward your opponent at a moment when your instincts will be urging you to flee. Aikido is based on centripetal force. The principle of *irimi* (pronounced like my home town of "Erie" and "me") refers to the fact that if you want to immobilize a stronger fighter, you have to get close enough to touch them. And if you want to solve a problem, you have to start by moving closer to it, something that takes great courage. In this chapter, we'll talk about why it's so important to attack the heart of a problem rather than getting distracted by tangents—and I'll explain how to tell the one from the other.

## Chapter 7. 呼吸 Kokyu: *Breath-Power*

Every aikido class begins and ends with an exercise called *kokyu-ho* (pronounced, koh-Q-hoe). You grasp a partner's wrists and hold on to each other while you each try to throw the other off balance, powered by nothing more than an exhaled breath. Students have to learn to relax their bodies—and also their minds. They have to learn not to worry about who looks silly, or who has practiced longer, or who is stronger; they have to stay focused only on their breath to avoid telegraphing their intentions. We all hold back in life because we are afraid of failing, afraid of looking silly, afraid of change. In this chapter, I will discuss how developing your own natural "breath-power" will help you let go of your ego and your fear of losing—and how that will clear the path to success.

## Chapter 8. 合気 Aiki: *Unity*

*Aiki* (eye-key) means "the harmonious meeting of energies." Students of aikido are following a time-honored path that involves learning to blend your energy with your opponent's, instead of trying to overpower them. Adepts who exhibits aiki never meet force with force. They assess their own abilities, and their opponent's, with clear eyes. They face their weaknesses and look for ways to use leverage to turn them into strengths. In this chapter, I'll show you how to clearly assess your own strengths and weaknesses, and how to look for ways to blend with obstacles, instead of trying to meet force with force.

## Chapter 9. 残心 Zanshin: *Calm Awareness*

*Zanshin* (zahn-sheen) refers to a preternatural state where you are calmly aware of absolutely everything around you, the way a warrior must be aware of the entire battlefield in order to survive. It builds on mushin. It's crucial not only in a life-or-death situation like a battle, but any time you need to make a decision. In this chapter, I'll explain how moving into a state of zanshin can help you see the true nature of your choice, understand the consequences of the decision you're about to make, and act decisively.

## Chapter 10. 和 Wa: *Harmony*

Aikido asks practitioners to approach battle with a radically different mind-set than the one most of us have been taught. You are not competing with others; you are striving for harmony, or *wa*. That is the secret to true victory in any situation—but most of us think of battle, and business, as dog-eat-dog and winner-take-all. In this chapter, I will show readers how taking this countercultural approach can become a differentiating strength. I'll also explain that seeking harmony doesn't mean being passive or putting aside your own needs. In aikido, harmony is achieved when you know how to protect everyone—including yourself.

## Conclusion. 澄み切り Sumi-Kiri: *Clarity of Mind and Body*

Finally, I'll close the book by talking about what it looks like when you combine all of these principles into a total clarity of mind and body. *Sumi-kiri* (sue-me-key-rhee) is a martial arts term that means "cutting through the clutter." It's the ability to find your calm energy, hold on to your one-point, achieve mushin, and see the essential heart of a problem with zanshin. It is the sum of everything we have talked about in the book: the almost supernatural clarity of mind and body that allowed Master Ueshiba to dodge bullets.

## HOW TO USE THIS BOOK

Achieving this kind of total clarity takes time, of course; however, it's a practice you can begin, and start reaping the benefits of, today—right now. This book will show you how. I'll be using personal stories to help you understand these concepts by showing you the journey I've taken to come to understand them. My goal is to help you see the world the way I see it and understand what I've gone through and how I approach problems so that you can gain the benefits of these wonderful principles. I urge you to read these stories and reflect on how you might apply the lessons in your own life. I'll also be asking you questions and sharing proven tools and techniques to help jump-start your thinking, progress, and success.

This book is organized so that the principles you'll learn about will build upon each other. We'll start with some of the simplest concepts—equanimity, energy, and balance—just as an aikido class would start with a simple meditation exercise to quiet the mind, and then focus on the core physical disciplines of directing your energy and holding to your center of balance. With that foundation established, we'll move on to some of the more advanced concepts. These principles will build upon one another. You can't achieve mushin without first understanding heiki, and you can't find zanshin without first finding mushin. Ultimately, we'll be working our way toward sumi-kiri: the total clarity of mind and body.

In each chapter, I'll give you practical exercises, tips, and techniques for you to implement. These are not "life-hacks." There is no shortcut to clarity, making better decisions, and peak performance. However, the tips and techniques are designed for you to use immediately and gain many benefits that will help you on your path to productivity, balance, and success. Give them a try. I hope you'll find that each tip or exercise helps push your thinking further and improves your day-to-day life. To dig deeper into these principles and extend your practice beyond the pages of this book, you can always go to my website, michaelveltri.com/book, to find the latest tips, techniques, videos, and updates.

You must combine the right spirit with the right behavior to truly transform your life. If you don't truly love what you do in all aspects of your life, no tips, techniques, or advice can help you succeed. This book may push you to think about whether or not you are truly in the right place in your life—whether you are doing what you are meant to do in your work and whether you are spending your time with the right people in order to truly be your best. If thinking this way makes you uncomfortable—good! I urge you to push through that discomfort and find your true path. Only then can you achieve peak performance in all areas of your life.

Peak performance and total clarity is a noble and challenging goal. You'll approach it again and again, only to see it slip through your fingers, grab it again, then drop it once more. My hope is that, by the end of this book, you will have obtained a clearer vision of yourself, what "success" means to you, and be well on your way to achieving more abundance, balance, and joy. You may not be able to dodge bullets like Master Ueshiba did, but you will be able to make better decisions, focus on what truly matters, and stay true to yourself.

Let's get started.

# CHAPTER 1

# 平気 *Heiki: Equanimity*

*This chapter will explore how entering into a state of equanimity, remaining calm under duress, prepares you to take action. You'll learn how crucial remaining calm is—whether in a crisis or just managing everyday situations. You'll see how summoning this calm energy, known as* heiki, *can help you see new solutions to a seemingly unsolvable problem. You'll read about some examples of people who have demonstrated heiki, and you'll be given some exercises to work on developing your own calm energy.*

Your boss just tapped you on the shoulder and said, "Hey—you got a minute? We need to talk for a second. . . ."

What runs through your mind when you hear those words? Does your heart start to race? Do you start imagining disaster scenarios? Counting up all your past sins? Do you think to yourself, "Oh, no, here we go again"?

Any of these responses would be perfectly natural—but none of them are particularly helpful. You know that you don't do your best thinking when panicking. You know that you can't have a healthy, helpful conversation with your boss, colleague, or loved one when you've got your hackles up. But what's the alternative? How can you escape the trap set by your own nervous system?

## There Is Another Way

The alternative is a state of mind and body known as *heiki*. It's a calmness under duress that you can practice deliberately—when you're triggered by an unexpected call or e-mail, facing a tough decision, or in the middle of some kind of crisis. I start each aikido martial arts class that I teach with a moment of meditation. This moment of quiet contemplation puts us in the right frame of mind to fight. Meditation and breathing exercises lead us toward that state of equanimity, or heiki (pronounced "hey-key").

The word *heiki* is made up of two characters: *hei*, meaning "calm, flat, or peaceful," and *ki*, which means "energy." Ki is also the center of the word *aikido*. Ultimately aikido is all about energy—balancing it, channeling it, harmonizing yours with your opponent's. In order to accomplish this, we start from a place of heiki—calm energy.

Aikido is a unique grappling art known as meditation in motion. The discipline requires you to remain calm in the face of adversity. Some martial arts ask you to go a bit out of control and release a lot of violent energy—yelling, kicking, and punching. In aikido, we must retain control. It's not about being passive or gentle—it's about letting go of fear, passion, and other artifacts of the ego.

This process of letting go of what we think and feel helps us open our minds to what the situation truly is. If you begin a bout with a desire to prove yourself or humiliate the other person, you're limiting what you'll be able to see. You'll see a threat, or you'll see an opening for a really cool move, instead of clearly seeing how your opponent is moving and what opportunities you have in the spaces created by their movements.

The same is true in our personal and professional lives. If you begin an argument or a negotiation mired in passionate emotion, you won't see the situation clearly. You won't see the other person as they truly are, and you will miss the multitude of true opportunities that are right in front of you. If, instead, you can remain calm, you'll be able to see many paths that wouldn't be available to you if you were angry, sad, upset, or out of control. Calm energy, heiki, provides access to opportunities you might not otherwise see.

## AN OPPORTUNITY TO PREVENT VIOLENCE

In May of 2013, Ingrid Loyau-Kennett was on her way home on the number 53 bus through London when she saw what she thought was a traffic accident.[1] Without stopping to think much about it, she got off the bus to see if she could help provide first aid to the victim.[2] But the situation she was walking into was no mere accident—it was a knife attack on a British soldier by terrorists who believed they were exacting vengeance for Britain's involvement in wars in the Middle East.[3]

Loyau-Kennett went straight to the victim and felt for his pulse. Almost the second she realized he was dead, she was confronted by one of the attackers. He was holding a gun and a meat cleaver in his bloody hands.

What would you do in that situation? Would you panic? Run away? Try to hit or kick the attacker, take away his weapons?

There were dozens of people standing in the street that day. Almost none of them made a move to help or interfere in any way. Some of them took pictures or shot video with their phones.

Loyau-Kennett stood up and faced the killer. "I didn't have any adrenalin at this moment," she has said. "Instinctively, and through my scout training, I like to keep calm and be respectful."

So she spoke calmly to him. She asked him questions—why had he done this? What did he want? Her goal was to keep this man talking, keep him from attacking anyone else. She could see there were children among the crowd watching the scene, and she thought, if he's going to attack anyone else, better me than one of these kids.

## A TRUE HERO

Loyau-Kennett may well have saved lives that day. But she doesn't believe that she did anything special. She thinks anybody could have done what she did.

I agree—anyone *could* have done that. But of course, most people wouldn't. Most people would be too afraid, too shocked, too angry, too something, to confront someone so obviously dangerous. Most people wouldn't have seen the path that Loyau-Kennett saw. Most people wouldn't have been able to imagine that asking a few simple questions could keep a situation like that from spiraling further out of control. But Loyau-Kennett was able to call on an inner reservoir of calm, and that calm energy allowed her to see a path nobody else could see.

In interviews, Loyau-Kennett has attributed her extraordinary heiki on that day to her Catholic faith.[4] That faith helped her see beyond herself, beyond the physical danger she was in, and focus on engaging with the attacker. Her faith helped her to let go of her fear and allowed her to perform an act of great courage— without even thinking of it as something out of the ordinary.

Courage doesn't require religious faith. There are many ways to reach that state of calm energy. But I believe that Loyau-Kennett's faith was invaluable to her in that moment because it took her outside of herself. It gave her a perspective and a purpose that was greater than she was. And that is the nature of heiki—calm energy derives from letting go of attachment, letting go of fear, letting go of all feelings about the self. Exactly how you find your way to that state of detachment and calm doesn't matter—what matters is that you find that calm place and operate from within it. When you do, like Ingrid Loyau-Kennett, you will see a new way out of a difficult or even dangerous situation.

## Calm Courage in the Everyday

Thankfully, most of us don't face down murderers every day. Most of us face more pedestrian challenges: a fight with a spouse, a negative review from a boss, a looming deadline at work. Summoning heiki can be just as useful in our daily lives as it is in a life-changing moment like the one Loyau-Kennett faced when she got off that number 53 bus. In fact, in some ways, finding equanimity can be even more difficult in a small moment than in a huge one. After all, when are you more likely to take a moment to clear your head before speaking—when you're facing a crisis, or when a colleague walks into your office to ask for an update on a project?

It's all too easy to get caught up in the wash of events in daily life. Most of us, most of the time, have "monkey mind"—we're constantly jumping from thought to thought, worry to worry. In today's world of constant interruptions, it's understandable—but it makes us likely to miss out on opportunities to change things or make real progress. When you approach a situation mired in your all-too-human emotions—stress, pain, fear, envy, excitement—you will only see that situation from your own perspective. You'll be thinking about how you need to defend your turf, justify your actions, get credit for your hard work, and so on.

When you approach a situation in a spirit of heiki, on the other hand, you'll see that situation from a kind of dispassionate bird's-eye view. You'll see more opportunities because you'll be thinking about everyone's needs and desires, not just your own.

I have a daily meditation practice that I will share with you very soon. And yet I still struggle to find equanimity in my daily life and work. Finding heiki in the midst of the bustle and business of everyday life is practice we must work at. And it's an incredibly powerful and beneficial practice. Heiki can become a knife that will cut through the toughest knots you're trying to untie in your personal or professional life.

## A MOMENT WHEN I NEEDED HEIKI

A few years ago, I made a big change in my life, both personal and professional. I moved from the East Coast to the West, and I started to focus more of my energy on expanding my executive coaching, consulting, and speaking business. That meant that I had to start handing over the daily operation of my successful aikido academy to other people.

This was a huge challenge for me. I am a take-charge, type A kind of person. I was a Marine, after all. I'm not used to stepping back and letting someone else do the work. So instead of simply appointing a successor and handing over the reins to that person, I found a second-in-command to take over most of the day-to-day running of the business—and I also brought in a friend of mine to teach one key class.

This friend, Greg, is a very nice guy, and he's very good at what he does. He had more expertise than my second-in-command, Jason, in this specific aspect of aikido. In fact, because he studied it exclusively, he had more experience than even I did in this particular area. I have a broader expertise in aikido overall, but Greg is really steeped in this one area of aikido.

So what could go wrong? Well, over time, the wrongness of this choice became more and more clear. Greg is an excellent practitioner in the area of his expertise, and he delivered clear and useful lessons in this technique for my students. But while the content of his lessons was great, he wasn't delivering those lessons in the right context.

---

### The Mushin Way Peak Performance Tip

If you have more than one e-mail address, consolidate to one—or at the most, one business and one personal address. Checking one e-mail address takes enough time out of your day—don't ruin your equanimity by trying to keep up with multiple ones.

---

The broader philosophy that underpins aikido—the idea that this is the martial art of meditation in motion, that your attitude and your intentions matter as much as your technique—is, to me, incredibly important. I want my students to walk away from my classes knowing not just how to move but how to think. My aikido academy appeals to high-achieving, driven people like me precisely because I don't just teach physical exercises. At my school, aikido is a way of life.

Greg wasn't delivering this philosophy in his lessons. At any other school, that would be fine. But at my academy, his lessons were confusing the message I wanted to deliver. Plus, assigning this key class to Greg was undermining my second-in-command, Jason. It sent a message to the staff and students that I didn't quite trust Jason to take over my role. Keeping my friend Greg on to teach that class was stunting Jason's growth as a young black belt. It was keeping him from growing fully into the new role I claimed I wanted for him.

Relying on my friend to teach this one class was a crutch—an easy way out. It allowed me to avoid doing the hard work of mentoring Jason to help him develop in his new role. And the longer I kept Greg around, the more he came to rely on this class as a crutch in his own life. He needed to push himself to develop his own business, but instead, he was coasting along, letting the money he was earning at my school tide him over, holding back on taking the next step.

I let this situation go on much too long. It wasn't good for any of us—but it was good enough, and I was busy enough, that I kept putting off doing something about it. But all the while, I was doing something else useful—I was creating structures of support around myself that helped me to come to clarity and take relevant action. I was surrounding myself with people who had my back, whom I could talk to and lean on. I was organizing my life in a way that would minimize distractions as much as possible and help me focus on my real priorities. And finally, I was ready to take action.

Greg and I sat down face-to-face and had a direct and open conversation. I explained why I felt it was time for him to leave the school—and he understood. He was disappointed, and I felt sorry about that, but ultimately the conversation was successful. He had been settling for part-time work when he should have been building a real business, and he knew that. In the end, having this tough conversation allowed us both to be more true to ourselves.

None of that would have been possible if I hadn't been coming from a foundation of heiki. If I had been coming from a place of fear or ego, I would have ended up avoiding the tough conversation, or yelling at Greg and having a huge falling out to cover my own failings.

## CALM ENERGY LEADS TO ACTION

Calm energy may sound passive, but it's not. In fact, heiki is a necessary foundation for relevant action. Without it, you'll end up like me—putting off that tough conversation—or like my friend Phillip, who takes putting off tough conversations to the absolute extreme. Phillip never breaks up with his girlfriends. He just coasts along, putting in little effort, until the relationship dies a slow, painful death. He lets his fear of that tough conversation make him passive. He's so afraid of how the women in his life might react to the truth that he can't see that he's making things worse for both parties. He can't find heiki because he's consumed by his fear—and so he's stuck in awkward inaction.

Heiki is not passive. Calm energy can be active energy—but it's an energy that's centered and dispassionate. Finding heiki was the first step toward resolving this situation. Once I found heiki, I was able to have a conversation with my friend Greg in which I genuinely sought a win-win-win solution—a win for me, a win for my business, and a win for Greg. Instead of acting out of my fear of hurting him, my irritation at the way my academy's message was being diluted, or my disappointment with myself for letting the situation go on for so long, I acted out of a state of equanimity.

Calm energy is incredibly powerful in everyday life. It helps you focus on what's important and screen out everything that isn't. That's why I start my aikido classes with a breathing exercise or a moment of meditation. I often recite a portion of what's called the Heart Sutra,[5] one of the foundational texts in Zen Buddhism. Here's a taste:

> This Body itself is Emptiness and Emptiness itself is this Body. This Body is not other than Emptiness and Emptiness is not other than this Body.

What does the idea of emptiness trigger in you? Do these words make you feel ready for action? Or do they make you feel something else?

The language of the chant is simple, but the ideas it describes can take a while to truly understand. This sutra gets at the heart of Zen Buddhism—the paradoxical idea that joy and pain are both traps for the mind, that we achieve enlightenment only by letting go of attachment. These are complex, contradictory ideas that monks spend lifetimes studying—but calm energy is also an actionable idea that you can start working toward today.

Whether on the feudal battlefield of Japan or the corporate "battlefield" of boardrooms around the world, detachment may not sound like the kind of focus you need to succeed. However, heiki establishes the foundation for clarity and relevant action. Heiki puts you in a frame of mind that opens your eyes to possibilities. Operating out of emotion closes our eyes and keeps us locked into unhealthy or unproductive patterns of behavior.

One simple way to start developing heiki is by starting a very simple and effective meditation practice. Meditation also has numerous proven health benefits. Research has shown that meditation increases brain activity in areas related to dealing with stress, focus, and remaining calm. Even trying meditation for a couple of days has lasting effects in reducing harmful inflammation.[6]

## Give This a Try

Here is one simple technique taken from my martial arts practice that you can try today to begin receiving the many benefits of mindful meditation. And it will only take you about one minute:

1. Sit up straight at your office desk before starting work—shoulders back and spine erect.

2. Close your eyes slightly. Leave them open a little bit so you can see a blurry image and some light (this will help prevent sleepiness).

3. Breathing in and out through your nose, take five deep breaths while expanding your belly. Count each breath as you exhale.

So you're breathing in and out, expanding your belly. While exhaling through your nose, count silently to yourself "one." Breathe in and out, silently counting "two" when you exhale. Keep going, counting up to five exhalations. Then stop. Open your eyes. And start your day. On average, each in-and-out breath sequence takes about 10 seconds. So the entire mindful meditation technique will take around one minute to complete.

Simple enough, right? Try this for a week, Monday through Friday, before you start work, when you finish work, and before you go to bed. This will only take about three and a half minutes to do. I know you can do it. I guarantee you will start to gain the benefits mentioned above, plus a whole lot more.

Heiki is a skill like any other. Careful practice of exercises like this can help you learn to find and hold onto the calm energy that positions us to see new possibilities and take relevant action, whether in a crisis, or in the fog of everyday life.

I encourage you to start practicing this crucial skill. Take a few minutes every day to do an exercise like the one I just described. You'll start seeing the benefits very quickly. Having a practice that puts you in touch with heiki on a regular basis will help you find that state of equanimity when you need it. In a crisis, when you're looking for your calm energy, you will now know what that calm energy feels like.

## THERE WHEN YOU NEED IT

Bill McNabb has terrible timing. He took the job as CEO of Vanguard Group at the end of August 2008—just two weeks before Lehman Brothers declared bankruptcy,[7] sending the stock market over a cliff and throwing the financial industry into chaos.

At a moment when many investors, including professionals, were panicking, McNabb stayed calm. His behavior was a perfect demonstration of heiki: He didn't react out of fear, but he wasn't passive, either. He joined other senior staff in getting on the phones to talk directly to investors. He also appeared in a video on Vanguard's website, talking clearly about the situation in the markets.

McNabb and other leaders at Vanguard displayed heiki during this crisis not only in the way they interacted with investors, but in the way they steered the company through the next couple of years. McNabb took the financial crisis as an opportunity to expand the company. This equanimity paid off: Investors flocked to Vanguard's funds. From 2008 to 2015, the company nearly tripled its assets under management.[8] It's now the biggest fund company in the world,[9] moving actively to expand overseas.

## EMBRACING HEIKI

Heiki is built into the corporate culture at Vanguard Group. Since 1987, Vanguard has had a team of volunteers from all across the company who are trained and ready to jump on the phones whenever something unusual happens in the market.[10] Inside the company, they're known as the "Swiss Army." There's even a red-and-white flag that flies when the Swiss Army is called to duty.

With this team of volunteers, and with its consistent messages to investors, Vanguard has carefully cultivated a spirit of heiki over the years. This calm attitude starts at the top and carries throughout the company. They market themselves as a company built for long-term investors, and they continually reinforce the message that investors should not panic when the market wavers. Because they routinely practice and reinforce equanimity, it's there when they need it. In a crisis, their "Swiss Army" team is ready to take action.

> ### The Mushin Way Peak Performance Tip
>
> When giving "lists," verbal or written, only give three pieces of information. The human brain can only remember three at a time—when you introduce a fourth item, the first one is pushed out of your mind.

Steady practice is key to developing your heiki. You can't expect to keep your head in a crisis if you've never practiced finding equanimity. As it is for the folks at Vanguard, cultivating calm energy needs to be a part of your daily plan as well as your crisis management plan.

For those who embrace it, heiki can become a key differentiator—as it is for Vanguard. Steady, calm management with a long-term focus is what Vanguard is known for. Heiki is part of their brand. And that brand has made them one of the most consistently successful companies in a highly competitive and volatile industry. What could happen for you if you made heiki part of your personal brand?

## WHEN YOU'RE KNOWN FOR FIGHTING FIRES, YOU GET MORE FIRES TO FIGHT

Red Adair saw his first oil-well fire when he was just six years old.[11] A lot of kids would be terrified by such a sight. The flames from an oil-well fire can reach hundreds of feet in the air. Temperatures near these fires can get hot enough to melt sand.[12] An exploding oil well creates an enormous amount of noise. It shakes the ground.[13] It's an apocalyptic scene. The six-year-old Red Adair responded to his first sight of such an overwhelming fire with a plan to put it out. He told friends he could handle it if he had a truck as big as a house.

Eventually, Adair got his chance to try his theory. After a stint in the Army, during which he worked in bomb disposal, he went to work as a firefighter. In 1959, he founded his own company. He became famous—John Wayne played him in the movie *Hellfighter*—for his ability to stay cool in what most people would see as literally hellish conditions. He seemed to relish the chance to attack out-of-control wells that were gushing oil and burning with intensely hot flames.

He was brave—that's obvious. But he denied he was a daredevil. He said to his biographer: "People call me a daredevil but they don't understand. A daredevil's reckless, and that ain't me. The devil's down in that hole and I've seen what he can do, and I'm not darin' him at all. I'm a beware-devil, that's what I am."

In his own colorful language, I believe that Adair was saying that his courage came not from heedlessly rushing into danger, but from caution. What he calls being a "beware-devil," I would call heiki—equanimity in the face of danger. Adair prided himself on his firm's safety record. He was there to contain the fire and keep everyone safe, not to get some kind of thrill from risking his life.

In 1991, during the first Gulf War, Adair was called in to fight oil fires in Kuwait.[14] The retreating Iraqis had left more than 600 oil wells burning. It was a massive job that would require water to be pumped in from the sea, sometimes as far as 100 miles. Undaunted, Adair told reporters at the time, "It's like other jobs, except there are more wells." Adair spent his seventy-sixth birthday fighting those fires. Thanks to his company's work, a job that many had expected could take as long as five years was done in nine months.

When you're as good as Adair was at fighting fires, your reward is more fires to fight. It seems that having a job to do was all the reward Adair wanted. Can you say the same?

## HELPING OTHERS THROUGH HEIKI

I'm no Hellfighter, but I am known for my heiki. My students and clients come to me for advice because they know that I've built my life around cultivating the kind of calm energy that creates a foundation for decisive action. And that's exactly why my client

Daniel came to me for advice when he got a very interesting job offer.

Daniel was a high-powered, high-achieving type of guy. He was an academic who had done some very important research. His work influenced policymakers, and he traveled in some very influential circles in his hometown. He'd been working for a while with a major Fortune 100 company, advising them on a few issues, when they approached him with an unexpected offer.

They asked him to come and work for them, setting up a new division that would use his research to develop new products and refine existing programs. They guaranteed he would earn millions of dollars. They flattered him. They told him they needed his expertise. They painted a picture of a fabulous new life of wealth and influence.

Daniel took an interview with them. He took a couple of interviews. And then he came to me. Over beers one evening, he told me he was really struggling with this decision. He loved his work at the university and he believed he was doing real good. But the corporate offer was tempting—he didn't hate the idea of experiencing a whole new type of power. He was torn. "What's the Mushin Way in this situation?" he asked me.

### The Mushin Way Peak Performance Tip

Walking 30 minutes a day helps reduce heart disease by 30 to 40 percent. Figure out ways to make it happen: Walk during lunch, while on the phone, or before or after your workday.

I could see that Daniel was in desperate need of some heiki. I talked him through the situation, asking him questions that pushed him to look at the situation from different angles. My questions helped Daniel slow down, take a breath, and find his equanimity. Slowly, he started to zoom out from the limited perspective of his ego and his fears, and see the situation more clearly, with the wider vision that calm energy provides.

Once he was able to pause and cultivate some heiki, Daniel realized that he didn't want to take this new position. He loved his work. It was his true calling. But he had started to feel guilty about going so far in his talks with this corporation—he felt like he had been wasting their time. He was afraid of disappointing them by saying no.

Heiki helped to bring him back to his center. When he embraced heiki, Daniel was able to see things from the corporation's perspective as well as his own. He realized that taking a job he didn't really want and would be unhappy doing wasn't good for anyone—a fact that his ego and fear had kept him from seeing. He had to get past that fear-based tunnel vision in order to see a completely new possibility, one that would be a win for everyone involved. After our conversation, Daniel went back to the company and turned down the job—but offered to consult with them on some of the new initiatives they were pursuing.

Trapped in the tunnel vision created by his ego, Daniel could only see an either-or choice: Take the job he wasn't going to like, or disappoint a bunch of important people. Heiki helped him see another option, a both-and option. He ended up happier, and so did his friends at the corporation he continued to work with. And all it took was some equanimity.

Aikido is all about seeing through our opponents' eyes, and that starts with heiki. Heiki zooms us out from the narrow perspective offered by our own egos and helps us see the whole field of battle, from many different angles. It shows us new possibilities we wouldn't otherwise be able to see. Whether you're fighting a fire or simply making a tough decision, heiki will help you find your path through the fog.

## The Mushin Way Action Step: How to Apply Heiki—Equanimity

1. What is one decision you've been putting off making for a couple of days or weeks even? Pick something easy to practice with such as "I need to schedule my next dentist appointment" or "I have to check in with my financial planner" or "I have to schedule a call with my boss to discuss my project/promotion/raise/and so on."

   Write it down here (ebook readers, write it down in a separate notebook or journal):

   _____

   _____

2. Perform the breathing exercise described earlier and summarized below:

   a. Sit up straight, shoulders back and spine erect.

   b. Close your eyes slightly. Leave them open a little bit so you can see a "blurry" image.

   c. Breathing in and out through your nose, take five deep breaths while expanding your belly. Count each breath as you exhale.

3. Embracing heiki, make a *relevant* phone call right now—talk to a live human being—to move your goal stated in step 1 forward. I don't care what time it is or where you are. *Do it. Now.*

    The result of my phone call was: _____

    _____

4. Post your result, questions, or comments on my website at michaelveltri.com/book

# CHAPTER 2

## 気 *Ki: Energy*

*This chapter will explore the concept of* ki, *the life force that drives everything you do. You'll learn why strength alone is never enough, how strength can actually make you weak, and how aikido teaches us that the key to success is to channel your strength into productive directions through the proper forms and systems of support.*

My student David was 6 foot 4 and built like a tank. My students in general tend to be type A high achievers like me, but even in this driven crowd, he stood out. He worked for the National Counterterrorism Center (NCTC), an elite group of CIA officers, FBI agents, and military special forces that focuses on analyzing intelligence drawn from many sources to identify and nullify threats from around the world. David was also a diligent student of aikido. When you showed him a move, he got it. He seemed to be unstoppable.

Then he decided to go back to school and get an MBA—while continuing his high-stress work at NCTC and his studies of aikido with me. And then he found out he was getting a huge promotion. And the promotion meant moving to the Middle East. Oh, and his wife was pregnant with their first child.

Even for David, pulling off all of this at once was going to be a challenge. In day-to-day life, David was like a force of nature.

His physical size and strength, combined with his intelligence and his drive to succeed, made him stand out wherever he went. He was driven to do an exceptional job of everything he turned his hand to. But even a person with as much energy and power as David couldn't start a new job, move to a strange place, get a degree, and care for an infant, all at the same time, without help.

Help, in this case, had to mean a ground-up restructuring of David's entire life. Just making small changes at the margin, like hiring a cleaning service, wasn't going to cut it. David's powerful energy needed to be supported at every moment and channeled in the most productive directions.

## BUILDING A NEW ROUTINE TO EMBRACE CHANGE

The first step was to evaluate every aspect of his life, starting with how he was supporting his physical health. He had to take a close look at his sleep habits, his exercise routine, and his diet. Failing to take care of his body would hold him back.

The next thing David had to do was look at his daily schedule. Was he giving himself enough time to take care of himself physically? With a new baby on the way, sleep and spare time were going to be at a premium. David had to make sure that he was organizing his schedule to focus on his true priorities. Physical health had to come first; then, supporting his wife and his new child; then, excelling at his job and completing his course work. David had always been a type A guy who made careful schedules to map out his time, but he would need to rely on this skill more than ever now.

Of course, it's one thing to make a schedule and another thing to stick to it. The next step in David's overhaul was to set up support structures that would help him achieve his goals. Support structures can be physical. David could get some new equipment, like an activity tracker to help him keep up with his exercise regimen, or a blender to make some healthy green smoothies to keep his diet on track, for example. Support structures can also be organizational. David could keep his running shoes right next to the door to make rolling out of bed for a run as easy as possible, or reorganize his desk to make sure his class materials were always easy to find.

---

### The Mushin Way Peak Performance Tip

Consolidate all calendars—work, home, spouse's, children's—into one. Streamlining these systems will help you focus and calm your energy in the most productive direction possible.

---

Support structures can also be interpersonal. David had to have some honest conversations with his wife, his friends and family, and his colleagues. Even the most powerful of us need help at times. This was a moment when David needed to make sure the people in his life knew what kind of challenge he was facing and were on board, ready to support him. He'd need a whole team behind him to make this all work.

High achievers like David are like Formula One race cars—high-performance machines. An elite race car is beautifully built. Every inch of it is designed with an eye to speed. But even the best car can't win a race without high-quality fuel in its tank. And the faster the car, the harder the pit crew has to work to keep it running.

In aikido, we talk a lot about something called *ki*—that's the energy that drives your every movement. It's the fuel in your tank.

It's your life force, your power. It is a "multiplier." It's crucial—but it's not enough on its own. You still need your pit crew. You need to refuel periodically, change your tires, and you need that guy standing by with the fire extinguisher in case something goes wrong. You can't achieve anything without your ki, but you also can't achieve anything on ki alone.

## IT'S ALL ABOUT ENERGY

What exactly is ki? It's an elusive concept, at best. Understanding it is experiential—ki is a physical and spiritual energy that flows through your body. To truly understand it, you're going to have to get on your feet and move a little. We'll get to that in a moment.

Ki can be defined as "inner energy," "life force," or "energy flow." It's the middle character in the word *ai-ki-do*—the center of everything we do in the martial art of peace. One way of describing ki is "to be in the zone." You know what I mean—when everything is just going your way, working out perfectly for you. You wake up in the morning full of energy, excited to start your day. You smile at everyone you meet, and they can't help but smile back. You effortlessly move from project to project. Your deadlines are met with ease and creativity. You lead your team with a level of grace and clarity that draws the admiration of everyone around you. Life is easy. That is an example of ki.

Ki can also be described as "self-confidence" and "charisma." In the Marine Corps we called it "command presence." When someone else has a powerful ki, you can sense it. For example, you can actually feel the ki energy flowing from Martin Luther King, Jr. when you listen to his "I Have a Dream" speech. You feel that tingle going up your spine? That is ki.

## MY OWN ENCOUNTERS WITH KI

My drill instructors at Marine Corps boot camp had powerful ki. The armed forces would refer to that ki as "command presence," but the idea is the same. I remember the first time I met my drill instructors. There were three of them and 60 new, untrained recruits—a bunch of teenagers, eager to please, nervous, unsure of what they had gotten themselves into—emotionally, all over the map. It was the powerful, focused, and directed ki of our drill instructors that got us through those first difficult days.

You could sense their energy as they were standing there in front of the group. Ki can't be faked. We can sense it in others because we unconsciously pick up on the nonverbal cues signaling that this person is fully present in this moment and fully committed to what they're doing. Think about the weary, seen-it-all high school teacher who's marking time until summer vacation, or the boss who's clearly more worried about protecting his turf than getting good work done. You can feel when there's a disconnect between the person's spirit and their actions. It makes everyone in the room uncomfortable. But when spirit and action are aligned, it's powerful. It's compelling. All eyes are drawn to that person. That's ki.

Ki doesn't have to be loud or domineering. My drill instructors were—but that was the natural expression of their focused energy. For other people, focused and directed ki can be as soft as a whisper—but it's still just as powerful. I remember an influential lobbyist I met when I first moved back to Washington, DC after leaving Japan. This woman, Ann, was very soft-spoken and reserved in her demeanor, but in her own way she was at least as intimidating as my drill instructors. She wasn't harsh or aggressive at all, but she was a formidable person to face in a meeting, because she was so supremely focused and present.

She was confident without being arrogant. When she listened, you could feel that she was listening with her whole self.

---

### The Mushin Way Peak Performance Tip

Plan your day each morning before starting any work—including checking e-mail. Move forward any items from yesterday that need to be completed today, ensure today's schedule is correct, and write down three high-priority action items to complete that day.

---

Ann and my drill instructors were totally different in most ways, but what they had in common was a sense that they were in exactly the right place at exactly the right time—that they were passionately committed to what they were doing. That feeling radiated off of them, drawing people to them. You instinctively wanted to be close to them, wanted to join in whatever they were doing. Their belief was so powerful that it was infectious. That's the power of ki when it's properly channeled.

Ki is both spiritual and physical. You feel it in your body. In Western cultures, the closest equivalent to ki is something personal trainers call proprioception. The term *proprioception* comes from the Latin word *proprius*, meaning "individual," and "perception." So it's about perception of yourself—of your body. It's an awareness of where your body is in space and how it's moving. Proprioception can be defined as developing a "sixth sense" that allows you to constantly monitor the stimuli in your body regarding position, motion, and balance, which keeps you aware and in control of the way your life force is propelling your body through space.

In aikido, we develop our ki through specific physical exercises designed to make you aware of how your energy is flowing through your body. All these exercises begin with three principles: relax, extend, and center. Keep your body relaxed—not floppy, but loose, ready to move. Extend your limbs, directing your energy purposefully. And center yourself—find your center of gravity and stay grounded in it.

### Give This a Try

Here's a simple exercise you can do with a partner: Both of you should stand up. Have your partner pull on your wrist. If you do nothing, your partner should easily be able to pull you off balance. Try that first and see how it feels.

Next, shift your hip out and extend your leg, directing your energy—your ki—into the ground. If you do this right, keeping your body relaxed, extending your leg, and staying centered in your low center of gravity, your partner will not be able to pull you off balance. In fact, you'll be able to use your centered and directed energy to pull your partner toward you.

Try it! It may take you a few tries to make it work, but once you get it right, you'll feel in your body how powerful ki is. Simply by shifting your body slightly and purposefully directing your ki into the ground, you'll become unmovable. It's not about force or strength; it's about directing your energy and letting it flow in the most productive way.

## When It Feels Like Ki Deserts You

My battle with cancer seemed to go well at first. But then, a few months after my first successful surgery, my doctor told me my cancer had returned and spread to my lung. Just when I thought I was done with cancer, my fight was actually kicking into high gear. I worked with my doctors to attack the problem the way I would attack anything else in my life: with everything I had. My chemo treatments were particularly brutal. Five days a week, Monday to Friday, 8 AM to 2 PM. Practically a full-time job. And believe me, this is not a job you want to have.

My doctor told me chemo would "make me feel a little blah." He said that because he didn't want to tell me I was going to feel like I was dying. And in a way, I was. That's how you kill cancer cells—you reduce the entire body to near-death, hope you destroy all the cancer cells, and then, hopefully, bring the rest of the body back to life.

At that moment, life felt like it was slipping away. I thought my ki had completely abandoned me. I could barely drag myself out of bed in the morning. I felt like a zombie—like I was wrapped in cotton, cut off from the world. I couldn't eat. The power went out for a week and it hardly mattered—there was nothing in my fridge but the hypodermic needles I had to use to inject myself with medicine every night before I went to sleep.

Of course, my ki hadn't abandoned me—it was the only thing keeping me going. But I had lost the physical power I was used to having. Even after the chemo was over, I had to have a piece of my lung removed. I left the hospital in a wheelchair after that surgery because I didn't have the lung capacity to walk yet. I suddenly knew what it was going to be like to age. I couldn't go anywhere without an elevator. My mom had to help me with everything. I literally couldn't get out of bed or eat or go to the bathroom without help. It was humbling. It was terrifying.

## Kı Alone Is Not Enough

It was months until I was able to go for a run again. (And a few years before I ran my first marathon—with only one and a half lungs. But that's a story for another time.) And when I did start to exercise again, I realized my whole sense of my body—my proprioception—had changed. I had to relearn all sorts of things I had taken for granted.

This was the moment when I finally learned, in a physical, visceral way, one of the central lessons of aikido: that ki is crucial, but ki alone is not enough. My life force carried me through my cancer treatments, but it wouldn't have been enough on its own. I couldn't have made it through my recovery without my mom and my doctors and nurses. And when I began to practice aikido again, I couldn't rely on my ki or my physical strength alone to power me through the movements. I couldn't do the exercises the way I used to—I had to relearn the techniques with my new, weaker body. Without that missing piece of lung, I couldn't do the exercises wrong anymore.

Aikido teaches us that physical strength is never enough on its own. You might be the strongest fighter in your class, or your country, or even the world. But even that kind of strength can be overcome. Say you're facing one opponent, and then his buddy shows up. If you try to use your strength alone to defeat both of them, you're going to lose. But if you channel your ki into the right structure, you can find a way to win—say, by pushing one of your opponents into the other, giving you the moment you need to retreat (yes, an honorable retreat can be a victory, if it means you live to fight another day).

Aikido is about harnessing your strength, your ki, into the forms and structures that will lead to success. Aikido teaches that relying on strength alone can be dangerously seductive—it can lead you to forget to follow the proper forms. And if you do, when you reach a moment when strength alone is not enough, you will undoubtedly fail.

## WHEN STRENGTH SEDUCES YOU

Relying too heavily on your strength can lead to defeat in many different ways. Maybe you'll finally come up against an opponent who's even stronger than you. Maybe you'll lose your strength, like I did after chemo. Or maybe you'll simply defeat yourself.

Today, Facebook is one of the most powerful and influential companies out there. It's grown enormously since Mark Zuckerberg launched TheFacebook.com in 2004. By 2008, the site had 100 million users. By 2012, the site could boast 1 billion users—tenfold growth in just four years.[1] But even as the site has grown exponentially, rapidly becoming a part of the landscape of our everyday lives, it's been criticized again and again.

Over the years, the ubiquitous social network has repeatedly changed its privacy policies.[2] Most of these changes have eroded users' control over their own information—and most of them have been made without consulting users. A couple of high-profile missteps have dented the company's reputation. For example, in 2007 the company imposed a new service for advertisers called Beacon, which automatically shared users' purchases with their friends.[3] Facebook had to apologize and ultimately scrap the program after huge outcry from users. In 2010, when Facebook introduced a location-based check-in function called Places, it again had to apologize to users over privacy concerns.

This pattern has been repeated multiple times. It's easy to imagine how this happened. The company was growing so quickly; its founder was a new kind of celebrity; it suddenly seemed like literally everyone and their mother was a member. That kind of strength can be intoxicating. It's easy to imagine how the company's powerful ki could have seduced it into attempting to move forward on brute strength—to force users to advertise the products they bought to their friends, or to push forward a change that would allow users to share their friends' physical locations without first getting permission.

The lesson Facebook needs to learn is one of the key lessons of aikido: that strength unchecked can be dangerous. Strength harnessed to a sensible, supportive structure is the key to success.

## Understanding Kɪ Means Understanding Your Own Limits

In 2015, Jessica Williams was a rising star. As a popular correspondent on the hugely influential *Daily Show*, clips and GIFs of her sharpest moments were all over the Internet. And then Jon Stewart announced that he was stepping down from his job as host. The world immediately started speculating about who would replace him—and Williams's name kept coming up.[4]

The idea of Williams as the new host of the show was popular with fans online. Some even started a petition asking Comedy Central to give her the job.[5] The petition got 14,000 signatures. A clip from the movie *Hot Tub Time Machine 2* showed Williams hosting the show in the future.[6] It seemed like the whole world was on board with the idea of Williams taking the host's chair.

Except, it turned out, Williams herself. Taking to Twitter, she explained that she was "underqualified for the job." She said, "At this age (25) if something happens politically that I don't agree with, I need to go to my room and like not come out for, like, 7 days." She noted that she was only beginning her career and wasn't planning on going anywhere. With grace, and gratitude for her fans' support, Williams made it clear that she didn't feel ready to take on this high-profile job. After all, she was only 25 years old. She had plenty of time to build her career in a more steady, sustainable way.

> ### The Mushin Way Peak Performance Tip
> We all suffer from "decision fatigue"—the inability to make good decisions as the day progresses. Plan your important decision making early on in your day. Leave menial tasks and errands for later in the day.

Her tweets also revealed a clear-eyed awareness of her own strengths and weaknesses. She said that, at that moment, she felt too personally and emotionally invested in politics to take on the job of running a show that would make jokes about it day in and day out, no matter what happened.

Do you have that kind of self-awareness? If you had a chance to take a huge promotion, one that would land you in a high-profile, high-pressure role, would you take the time to think carefully about whether it was the right choice? Or would you jump straight in, seduced by the idea that someone saw you in such a flattering light? In Chapter 1, I talked about a time when my student Daniel faced a similar dilemma. Like Daniel, Jessica Williams also needed to draw on calm energy—heiki—in order to make the right decision.

If you were relying on your strength and energy alone, you would leap into a new role without thinking through all the possible outcomes. Strength can be seductive. It has to be married to the proper forms and structures in order to create success. Ki, in aikido, is about that powerful life energy that pushes us all forward; but it's also about that awareness of yourself and where you are in space, that sixth sense that trainers call proprioception. When it comes to your career, this kind of awareness will help you see which opportunities are right for you—and which aren't.

## Learning Self-Awareness As an Entrepreneur

Several years ago, I followed the common business advice of the day to "pursue your passion." I left a very safe, secure, and well-paying job in corporate America to start a business doing something I was truly passionate about and very good at doing. That's the American dream, right? Find something you're truly passionate about, pursue it obsessively, and become wildly successful and wealthy, right?

All you have to do is work harder and longer than anyone else. Be smarter and stronger than everyone. Sacrifice everything to achieve your dream. And that is what I did. And I promptly started working longer and harder—and producing more mediocre results than I had ever produced before that led nowhere. It was a horrible experience. From the outside, I appeared successful—but in reality, I was successfully miserable.

Where did I go wrong?

I wasn't good at delegating. I didn't play well with others. I was afraid to let go. I cut myself off from the world, built a wall of to-do lists, and tried to use brute force to get through all the tasks necessary to run a new business. My biggest strength—my indomitable work ethic—had become a huge, crippling weakness.

I had to remember to practice what I preach. I had to remember the elegant principles I've spent my life studying. Once I started applying the principles of aikido to my business life—using ki as the game-changer, as a multiplier—the difference was almost instantaneous. I became better at hiring and training staff, learned to delegate efficiently, and learned to let go to achieve more. I worked on not letting my ego get in the way of my success. And it worked.

I've seen a lot of other entrepreneurs struggle with the same kinds of problems. They are killing themselves, working as hard as they possibly can, but they're not setting themselves up for success. They're setting themselves up to be successfully miserable. For example, I've seen a lot of entrepreneurs try to get a business off the ground while maintaining a "day job" that pays the bills, or even try to run two businesses at the same time—one that makes steady money and one that's more of a passion project. Trying to split your energy—your ki—between two projects is a way to set yourself up to fail. You won't be fully committed to either project. Of course, you have to be financially responsible, but there comes a point when you have to commit and find ways to build support structures and channel your ki in a way that sets you up to truly succeed.

## CHANNEL YOUR KI TO SUCCEED

On one of my recent trips to Japan, I was viscerally reminded of the way aikido teaches that strength alone is not enough to win when I worked out with my aikido master. I'm more than 20 years younger than him—stronger, faster, bigger. If we were arm wrestling, I would definitely win. But in our aikido bout, when I grabbed him, it was like trying to grab water—he flowed, relaxed, and moved effortlessly. Without his strength holding him back, he performed his aikido technique perfectly and tossed me about like a rag-doll. I was using too much strength, force, and effort, while my aikido teacher was channeling his energy through the proper forms—and he was far more successful as a result.

The more strength I used, the more tired I became. The more effort I exerted, the less successful I was. Does this sound familiar? Have you ever run into a situation, at work or at home, where the harder you try, the worse you do?

Sustainable success requires a huge sacrifice but not the sacrifice you might think. It's not about simply trying harder, applying more force to the problem, and pushing through on ki alone. Success requires the sacrifice of kicking our fears and ego to the curb to disrupt those weaknesses that are masquerading as strengths. And how do you get those fears and ego under control? Easy. You need inspiring support structures sufficient to ensure your success. You need to channel your ki in the most productive direction. You cannot succeed alone.

Let me repeat that: *You cannot succeed alone.*

## BUILDING ELEGANT SUPPORT STRUCTURES

There are two types of support structures—systems and people. Tony Robbins's mentor, Jim Rohn, was fond of saying, "You are the average of the five people you spend the most time with." Who are the five people you spend the most time with? And how can they help you overcome your fears, balance your ego, and help you see where your strengths are actually holding you back?

If these five people can't help you see yourself more clearly, you need to find the right people who will reflect your ki back to you. That doesn't necessarily mean cutting people out of your life, but it may mean reorganizing the way you spend your time in order to better reflect your true priorities.

Aside from people, what systems do you have in place to help you ensure you are able to clearly see where your strengths are holding you back, where you're trying to push through on *ki* alone? There are many types of systems. For example, your office is a system. If you don't like the environment of your office—the lighting, location, or layout—you are going to exert more effort to produce the same results. You may need to reorganize the system of your office to direct and support your ki in the most productive directions possible.

Technology is also a system—do you use technology, or does it use you? Are you constantly distracted by looking at your phone for that next ping? If so, again, your fear and ego are forcing you to work harder, with more effort, producing less satisfying results— all because your system is off kilter. If this sounds familiar, consider deleting e-mail and social media apps from your phone to cut down on distractions and create a system that channels your ki in a better direction.

## THE PAYOFF

When you have the proper support system, life feels easy, even if you're facing enormous challenges. You get into that state of flow that I talked about earlier in this chapter, where ki is flowing through you in perfect harmony instead of being blocked or misdirected. Instead of watching the clock, waiting for the end of the workday, you'll find you check the time and realize that hours have passed without your even noticing. And because your energy and your work are aligned, you'll find that you draw people to you more effortlessly than ever. People will sense the energy crackling through you, and they'll want to join your mission.

I've been lucky enough to feel this way a number of times throughout my life. For example, when I was in boot camp, life felt easy to me, in part because the proper structures were there to support and direct my energy in the right directions. Reveille woke me up every morning. Everyone around me was getting up at the same time, working as hard as I was. My day was structured for me. I knew exactly where I needed to be and what I needed to be doing at all times. My instructors and my comrades were all working together on the same project—the project of transforming all of us into Marines. My energy and my work were aligned, and the people around me were supporting me in my efforts. My ki was directed and channeled exactly as it needed to be.

You may not be in boot camp, but you can still set up your life to support and direct your energies in the directions that will help you achieve your goals. For example, say your goal is to lose weight. You'll need the support of the people around you, especially the people you live with. If your spouse keeps bringing home burgers and fries for dinner, or your roommate keeps baking brownies, it's going to be that much harder for you to meet your goal. You'll also need to create some support systems that will help channel your ki in the right directions—like joining a running group to keep you accountable to showing up to exercise regularly, or setting your workout clothes in a gym bag at the end of your bed so it's easy to get up and get going in the morning.

No matter what your goal is, you can and should create systems that will support you in achieving it. If you're building a business, find a mentor and join your local chamber of commerce. Enlist your friends and family to help you network, so they feel invested in your success. Or have them help you to relax, blow off steam, and de-stress. You can't power through to success on strength alone—you need support. You need to harness your ki so that you don't exhaust yourself and burn yourself out. That means understanding your limits, making sure to put yourself in the right places at the right times, and creating systems that will help channel your energy toward your goal.

## The Mushin Way Action Step: How to Apply Ki—Energy

1. List the five people you spend the most time with. After each person's name, write down why you enjoy spending time with them—what energy do you get from their ki? For example, Tom—my best friend who makes me laugh, gives me great advice when I need it, and helps me blow off steam. Monica—my boss. Great leader, amazing teacher, and super mentor.

   1. _____
      _____
      _____

   2. _____
      _____
      _____

   3. _____
      _____
      _____

   4. _____
      _____
      _____

   5. _____
      _____
      _____

2. Think: You are the average of the five people you spend the most time with. So now it is time to work the list—of the five people above, are there any who need to go? Should you replace one or more with someone else who

will support you in achieving your goals or who will be a positive influence in your life? Is there anyone else in your life you want to spend more time with?

3. Rewrite your Top 5 list below again listing who and why.

1. _____
   _____
   _____
   _____

2. _____
   _____
   _____
   _____

3. _____
   _____
   _____
   _____

4. _____
   _____
   _____
   _____

5. _____
   _____
   _____

4. What is another decision you've been putting off making—for a couple of days, weeks, or even months? Is it time to focus your energy and negotiate a 15 percent raise at work? What about finally asking that special person out on a date? You now have a list of five allies—an abundance of ki—to help you accomplish this goal.

   Use the space below to declare your goal ("I will get a raise of $10K per year" or "I will ask Monica out on a date") and get into relevant action to make it happen. *Do it. Now.*

(*continued*)

*(continued)*
Goal Declaration:

_____

_____

_____

5. And when you get stuck, call one of the five people listed above for help and support. Or get help from me and *The Mushin Way* community! Just leave a question or comment on my website at michaelveltri.com/book

# CHAPTER 3

# 結び *Musubi: Connection*

*In this chapter, we'll discuss the crucial importance of connection in business and in life. In aikido, we talk about* musubi *(pronounced moo-sue-bee), the powerful connection that enables us to see through our opponent's eyes and anticipate his next move. In this chapter, you'll learn how to cultivate this kind of connection and why it can make the difference between success and failure.*

In 1925, an officer in the Japanese navy came to Professor Morihei Ueshiba's dojo to challenge him in combat. Ueshiba, the founder of the martial art of aikido, was a master already. The previous year, he had faced death in the mountains and survived due to an astounding ability to sense what was happening around him. But this was another kind of challenge: an ordinary one-on-one fight, like dozens, if not hundreds of others both men had experienced over the course of their lives.

This naval officer was armed with a sword. Ueshiba faced him unarmed, standing before this skilled swordsman with nothing but his body and his calm mind. The swordsman attempted blow after blow. Each time he moved, Ueshiba moved, easily dodging his opponent's sword. The fight went on like this until the swordsman gave up, exhausted. The first and greatest master of aikido won this battle without striking a single blow.

Afterward, Ueshiba refused to gloat. "It was nothing," he said:

> Just a matter of clarity of mind and body. When the opponent attacked, I could see a flash of white light, the size of a pebble, flying before the sword. I could see clearly that when a white light gleamed, the sword would follow immediately. All I did was avoid the streams of white light.[1]

Sure. All he did was see his opponent's next move coming a moment before it happened. Anyone with the ability to see the future could do the same thing, right? Easy as pie.

Ueshiba's sword dodging may seem supernatural, but it's actually a natural ability that each of us has the potential to develop. Anyone who practices aikido will learn the core values and techniques that put Ueshiba on the path toward this moment. Learning to anticipate and see your opponents' moves—to feel them before they happen—is a completely achievable goal. You may not see streams of white light emanating from their swords, but you can learn to see through their eyes. And developing this valuable skill starts with one of the core concepts of aikido: *musubi*.

## TYING THINGS TOGETHER

Musubi is a simple Japanese word that, in everyday language, means "tying knots" or "tying things together." In aikido, it stands for a deep connection with yourself that enables you to connect to the natural world around you—and to your opponent. For Ueshiba, this connection became so powerful that it enabled him to literally see what was coming next. Of course, not all aikido students develop such a powerful sense of musubi. But connection is at the foundation of everything we do in aikido.

## Give This a Try

Here's a simple physical exercise you can do to develop musubi. You'll need a partner. The two of you should touch your wrists together, right wrist to right or left wrist to left. Your goal is to never lose that physical connection of wrist to wrist. Each of you should take turns being the lead for 30 seconds at a time. You'll move your arm back and forth, up and down, your partner will move with you. Then you'll switch, and you'll follow your partner. Don't lose that connection. Try switching hands, too. If you started with your right wrists, switch to the left.

If you want to increase your focus, up the stakes. Put a $1 or $5 bill (or a $10 or a $20!) between your wrists. If whoever's not in the lead loses the connection, the lead gets the money. Of course, it doesn't have to be money. You could create a "challenge note" and write down something that the loser has to do if they break the connection—wash the car, buy lunch or a round of drinks, pick up the dry cleaning, whatever's meaningful to the two of you. The idea is to focus on keeping that connection at all costs.

## It's All about Connection

Focusing on the principle of musubi has been useful for me in building several businesses. It's actually completely changed the way I hire people. I used to hire based on content. I would write out a job description and list the qualifications I thought the person in this position would need: a bachelor's degree, three years of experience in a similar position, and so on.

Hiring that way got me people like Alex. Alex had gone to college on a double athletic scholarship. He had a bachelor's degree in communications and a master's in sports management. He had experience developing youth sports programs, which was exactly what I was looking for at the time—someone to help build out my aikido academy's youth classes. On paper, it was a total home run. I met with him for an interview and we really hit it off. So I hired him.

Six months later, we both agreed it had been a horrible mistake. Alex's passion was baseball. He'd had great success in his previous job because he was building a youth baseball program, doing something he loved and giving a younger generation a chance to experience this game that meant so much to him. He was technically qualified for the position at my school, but his heart wasn't in it in the same way. He didn't have a passion for aikido, and that meant he didn't really fit in with the corporate culture I had created.

So, after six months, Alex and I parted ways. And this time, I advertised the position in a completely different way. Instead of hiring based on content, I hired for context. I advertised the position to my existing adult membership—everyone who was taking classes at my elite aikido academy. I didn't say anything about qualifications. I just said, "If you are passionate about aikido and passionate about the environment we are creating here, come talk to me." Instead of looking for the right resume, I was looking for musubi—that deep connection that can't be faked.

That's how I found Ryan, the person who has since become my trusted business partner and the executive director of my aikido academy. That's also how I've hired for other positions since then. And since I hired Ryan and started looking for musubi above all, our revenue has increased exponentially, creating the solid foundation that has allowed me to expand my coaching, consulting, and speaking business. Without that foundation of musubi, none of what I'm doing now in my business would be possible, such as writing this book!

> ## The Mushin Way Peak Performance Tip
> Remove wireless e-mail from your phone. I know you don't want to—but trust me, you need to. It's a distraction and it splits your focus. You don't need it. E-mail can wait until you're ready to deal with it.

It doesn't matter what position I'm hiring for. I believe everyone in an organization needs to have that same sense of connection to the place and to the mission, or the whole business will suffer.

Many of us have experienced a lack of this kind of connection from the employee's side. Without musubi, without a true, deep connection to the work that you're doing, going to the office is just a misery from start to finish. Your alarm goes off and you immediately feel that dread right in the pit of your stomach. You drag yourself out of bed. You yell at the other drivers on the road or seethe inwardly at that annoying guy taking up too much space on the train. You slump in your desk chair, you scroll through Facebook, you take a million coffee breaks, you do anything you can to avoid facing the reality that this is your job and you're stuck here until 5:00 PM.

As a business owner and entrepreneur, I don't want anyone working for me to feel that way. Even one person who lacks connection can drag the whole team down. That's why I now focus on musubi above all else when I hire people. If you have a passion for the work, you can learn everything else you need to know. If you lack that connection, you're always going to be struggling to fit in and to meet your goals.

## BUILDING MUSUBI: START WITH SELF-INTEREST

So how do you create this kind of connection, personally or professionally? Musubi starts with something I like to call enrollment. You can't lead a team through guilt, fear, or obligation. You have to enroll people in the mission you're pursuing. You have to connect them to that mission. And that begins with showing them the way the mission benefits them, so they are truly inspired to carry out their assigned tasks with excitement and passion.

We're all motivated, to some extent, by self-interest. Enrollment begins here—at the moment when we see what's in it for us. If you're managing a team at work, this step can be fairly simple. If the team does well, the company does well, and if the company does well, we all keep our jobs. Easy enough. But you'll create a more powerful sense of connection if you also show your team some less tangible benefits—acknowledgment for a job well done, the chance to do more challenging or interesting work, and so on. The key is to see the situation through their eyes—what would you want if you were in their shoes?

Many people lose this ability to see the world through their team's eyes once they get promoted into a managerial role. As a manager, you're suddenly responsible for the success or failure of the whole team. You're accountable for the team's bottom line. You're looking at a much bigger picture. It's easy to lose sight of what it's like to be an individual contributor. If you manage a team, it's crucial that you remember where you came from and maintain your ability to relate to each and every employee on your team. If you lose this ability, you'll lose the connection you need to your team.

You can create enrollment in your personal life, too. Say you've set yourself a goal of losing 20 pounds. This will mean some lifestyle changes—you'll need to get up early to go to the gym, which means you'll need to go to bed earlier. You'll need to cut out sweets, keep tempting snacks out of the house, and plan healthier meals. All of that affects your spouse, so you'll need to enroll them in your mission—and you can start with their simple self-interest. If you achieve your goal, you'll be happier and healthier. Maybe you'll feel more confident going out dancing with them. Again, look at the situation through their eyes and think about what would motivate them to enroll in your mission. When that alarm goes off at 5:00 AM, you want your spouse cheering you on, not grumbling about the early hour.

## DEEPENING THE CONNECTION

Of course, enrollment shouldn't stop there. Self-interest is too narrow to keep people motivated over the long haul. If you're leading a team at work, you need to help members see beyond their self-interest and get them enrolled in the company's broader mission. Researchers at Middlebury College in Vermont and the Institute for the Study of Labor in Bonn, Germany found that workers who believe in their company's mission produce 72 percent more than workers who don't.[2] We all need a sense of mission to keep us going.

Enrolling a team in a mission starts with your ability to appeal to their self-interest—but true musubi comes when you can persuade them to also see the situation through your eyes. You do this by opening up to them and allowing yourself to be transparent. Talk to the team about why meeting this quarter's goals is important to you. Maybe you need to prove that the team can take on a big challenge, so that you won't find yourselves broken up and shifted around to other parts of the organization. Maybe you had a conversation with a client or customer that really brought home to you that your team needs to do better at customer service. Maybe you spoke to someone who doesn't use your company's products and you saw an opportunity to change that person's life for the better.

Whatever it is, open up and talk about it. Show your team what the world looks like from where you sit—they will thank you for it. Keep in mind that if you are not completely transparent, honest, and open with your team, they will sniff it out in a millisecond, and your connection—your musubi—will be broken.

---

### The Mushin Way Peak Performance Tip

Hire a "virtual assistant" to help you achieve more, with less stress, throughout your day. Virtual assistants can do things you don't want to do or are not good at doing such as buying birthday, holiday, and anniversary presents; researching any number of business and personal subjects; or cleaning up your e-mail inbox each morning. Need recommendations on a good one? Check my website for ideas! michaelveltri.com/book

---

The same goes for enrollment on a personal level. Let's go back to that weight-loss example. Talking to your spouse about how you'll both benefit if you achieve your goal is a good start— but imagine how much more committed they'll be to supporting you if you're willing to open up and be vulnerable and talk about why this goal is important to you. Tell them how that extra weight affects your self-esteem and your confidence. Tell them you're afraid because of your family's history of heart disease. Tell them about your vision of the future and how losing this weight will make that future better. Let them see through your eyes why you're working toward this goal. Help them see how your interests can be aligned—exactly how the goal will benefit both of you. That's how you create a true connection.

Enrolling someone in an effort to achieve a common goal is one way to create musubi. It starts with your effort to see the world through the other person's eyes, and it is greatly strengthened when you show the other person how the world looks through your eyes. A true two-way connection like this is incredibly powerful. A team running on musubi is practically unstoppable.

## WORKING WITHOUT MUSUBI

A team without this kind of connection is doomed to failure. I've seen this happen many times. Far too many businesses fail to develop this kind of connection with their employees or their customers—and that failure comes at a significant cost.

Back in 1995, I was working as a consultant in Japan. Part of my work involved advising non-Japanese companies on how to set up branch offices in Japan. I'd help them hire bilingual staff and navigate cultural differences. I always advised companies to go into the Japanese market on their own—I learned that joint ventures were pretty much doomed to failure. There could be no true musubi between a Japanese company that's established in its own market and a foreign competitor trying to break in. The advantage is all on the Japanese company's side. The interests aren't truly aligned.

In 1995, at the Tokyo auto show, my Japanese colleague Hitoshi and I saw my theory about joint ventures proved perfectly. One of the Big Three American automakers was rolling out a new car for the Japanese market at the show. It had been produced in a joint venture with a major Japanese manufacturer. This car was one of the centerpieces of the show. The American manufacturer was putting a lot of marketing muscle behind it. And it was a total disaster.

Hitoshi and I checked out the car together. As we looked, he started listing everything that was wrong with it, and I started taking notes. I stopped writing after about 50 points. Everything, from the size of the seats to the layout of the dashboard, was wrong with this car. It was like the manufacturer had never even spoken to a Japanese person. They had no real connection to the market or the consumer they were trying to reach.

American automakers have repeatedly failed to make any real headway in the Japanese market. Protectionist tariffs play a role, of course, but commentators have also noted that American manufacturers just aren't making the kinds of cars Japanese people want to buy. They don't produce enough right-hand-drive vehicles,[3] for one thing. American cars are not energy-efficient enough. They're not styled to appeal to Japanese consumers. They stick out instead of blending in.[4] American automakers have never been able to establish the kind of connection to the Japanese consumer that they would need in order to sell cars in that market.

## YOU CAN'T SELL WITHOUT MUSUBI

How many times has this happened in your life? How many times have you tried to sell something to someone who just doesn't want it? Maybe you've felt this way at a job interview, where you can feel yourself desperately trying to twist your résumé to fit what the hiring manager seems to want. Maybe you've tried to sell yourself to a date by pretending you're into football or hiking or dog shows or whatever it is the person seems to want. Maybe you've tried to get a four-year-old to eat brussels sprouts. Whatever the situation, without a true two-way connection—without musubi—you're just not going to make that sale.

I use this principle of musubi all the time in my consulting and speaking business. If I went into an organization in the unconnected way that this American automaker went into Japan, I would never make a sale. I can't just walk into an organization with a laundry list of my programs and accomplishments. I need to look at the situation through their eyes and understand what problems they're facing. I need to connect to what they need before I can approach them as a potential partner.

The connection has to go both ways—I have to be able to see through their eyes, and I also have to be honestly representing myself. If what they need is "corporate entertainment"—a keynote speaker who is just going to entertain their senior VPs with the latest business clichés and fads—then I'm not going to be the right fit. I need to look for organizations that need what I can provide—a business transformation process that will create organizational clarity and lead to peak performance. In order to succeed as a keynote speaker, I have to truly connect with each person in the audience, whether I'm speaking to 10 people or 10,000 people. That means I have to be truly open, transparent, and authentic about what I'm trying to do—or the audience will be able to tell immediately that I'm not really connected to my message.

That's why it's so uncomfortable to sit across from a potential employer or partner and try to pretend you're someone you're not. Because that connection isn't going both ways. You've connected with them well enough to understand what they're looking for, but you've lost your connection to yourself. And that means you're blocking the other person from truly connecting with you as you really are.

## TURNING A COMPANY AROUND BY CULTIVATING CONNECTION

Anne Mulcahy took over as the CEO of Xerox at a pretty dark time for the company.[5] Xerox had been losing money for six years, and it looked like the company's next step would be into bankruptcy. A few years later, she had led a complete turnaround, paid off the company's debt, and brought it back to profitability. When she retired in 2009, the company was feeling the strain of the recession, but Mulcahy was still credited with the enormous success of pulling it out of its tailspin.[6]

How did she do it? Mulcahy's first step as CEO was to go on a 90-day listening tour, talking to people within the company and to customers about what was going wrong and how they could improve. According to news reports, she told employees, "I will fly anywhere to save any customer for Xerox."[7] She started with musubi. She started by rebuilding the connections between the company and its employees, and between the company and its customers. Even after the company returned to profitability, she continued to focus on client service as a top priority. And as a leader internally, she has said she focuses on hiring people who are a good fit with the company's culture and values, and on creating an environment that values honest feedback for employees.[8]

### The Mushin Way Peak Performance Tip

Coffee drinkers—good news! Coffee increases dopamine levels and lets you work out 10 to 15 percent longer. Plus, it helps cognitive function. Remember to drink coffee in moderation and to avoid the high-calorie, sugary coffee drinks.

Mulcahy came up through human resources, and she has said that experience taught her the crucial importance of open communication. I believe she succeeded in turning Xerox around largely because she valued communication and connection so highly. She valued musubi, and she was able to rebuild the connections the company needed to succeed.

Under Mulcahy, Xerox also refocused its efforts on sustainability.[9] The company worked on reducing waste and ensuring that its copiers could be "remanufactured," or completely recycled into new products. This effort reconnected the company to its own core values and the values of many of its customers. This represents another kind of musubi: a connection to yourself that anchors you in your true values and focuses you on your true long-term goals instead of short-term gains.

## PUTTING MUSUBI INTO ACTION

A few years ago, I was invited to start teaching aikido to staff at CIA headquarters and at the National Counterterrorism Center (NCTC), an elite, little-known organization that draws its members from the CIA, FBI, and military Special Forces. NCTC was created after the September 11 attacks to fight terrorism and prevent attacks before they happen. You've heard the expression "the tip of the spear"? Well, NCTC is the razor-sharp edge of the tip of that spear.

I taught aikido to men and women who were working some of the most challenging, dangerous jobs in the world. Some of them spent their lives in windowless rooms, analyzing intelligence reports. Some of them traveled constantly, working on the ground in foreign countries. For all of these people, musubi was one of the parts of our aikido lessons that resonated the most.

We talked a lot about musubi. Aikido is a grappling art. It's not like fighting with a weapon, where you're keeping your opponent at arm's length. It's not even like boxing, where you're primarily focused on striking your opponent. In aikido, you're in close contact with your opponent. Someone is grabbing you, and you have to be able to feel their strength, feel their resistance, and sense their intentions. You can't just impose your will on them. You have to develop that connection, that feeling, that allows you to surpass your ego, fear, and strength.

Connection is at the core of successful intelligence work. Analysts and other CIA officers have to able to connect and see through the eyes of the individuals and groups they're studying. This can be a huge challenge for them—after all, they spend their lives pursuing people who want to attack and harm the country they love. It would be easy for them to see these people only as alien enemies. You hear this kind of rhetoric all the time from politicians, unfortunately—terrorists are described as "evildoers" who "hate freedom." Any analysts who bought into this kind of simplistic, black-and-white view would have a very hard time predicting their target's next move. Instead, the men and women I worked with had to find a way to connect with their targets and understand them as people in order to understand their intentions and predict what they would do next.

Analysts and operatives also have to connect with one another. Analysts are the brainpower of the counterterrorism effort. They're brilliant, they're thoughtful, and they're careful. Operatives are the ones who do the work on the ground. They're courageous, committed, and willing to take risks. It would be easy for each group to dismiss the other. And yet it's crucial for these two groups to connect for success. They need to be able to see through each other's eyes. In the case of the CIA or NCTC, visceral application of musubi—connection to self and others—can literally save countless lives.

Any business needs to develop this type of deep connection between disparate groups of people—sales and tech support, management and the rank-and-file, and so on. If people working this kind of high-stakes, challenging, dangerous job can find strength and success through musubi, what might it be able to do for you? What would connecting more deeply with your colleagues allow you to accomplish? How could learning to see through your customers' eyes change your business? How would building a deeper connection with your friends, family, or spouse change your life?

## *The Mushin Way* Action Step: How to Apply Musubi—Connection

Musubi is about inspiring others to help you achieve a goal because they see the benefit for themselves. No one will help you accomplish anything out of guilt, obligation, force, or duty. For example, my sales team increased revenue by 37 percent in one quarter (my goal was only 30 percent, by the way) because each one of them received either more money in commissions or more flex time off if we hit the goal. They got to choose which one. We would never have achieved these results if I had just yelled and screamed like a madman for them to "hit their number" without making it worth their while. Results would have been mediocre at best.

1. What is one work-related goal you are trying to achieve—increase sales, get a promotion, find a new vocation?

*(continued)*

(*continued*)

Write it down here (e-Book readers, write it down in a separate notebook or journal):

Goal: _____

_____

2. Write down three or more people who can help you achieve this specific goal, or whose support you'll need to accomplish it. Reference your list of five people from the exercise at the end of Chapter 2 if necessary, then add others if you need them. Perhaps you need to network with a colleague from a previous job you have not spoken with for a few years. Write down three or more people below:

1. _____

_____

2. _____

_____

3. _____

_____

3. Now rewrite the list below, noting next to each person's name what specific benefits *they* stand to gain by helping you. For example, "My spouse will finally get the time off she wants and needs on the weekend because she is helping me accomplish (insert big, important goal) during the week." Write your list below:

1. _____

_____

2. _____

_____

3. _____

_____

4. Get into action. *Now.* I don't care what time it is or where you're at. Connect with everyone on your list—create true musubi. Talk to each person on your list—don't hide behind e-mail or texts—so they know what your goal is, why you are doing it, and why it will be beneficial for *them* to help you. Write your results below, and share any big wins, questions, or comments with me and *The Mushin Way* community at michaelveltri.com/book

# CHAPTER 4

## 念 Nen: One-Point

> *In this chapter, we will discuss how to stay centered in a world where you're constantly being pushed and pulled in all directions. You will learn how to find your life's "one-point," or center, by setting proper priorities for yourself, and you will learn physical and mental exercises that will help you stick to this center in good times and bad. We'll discuss how staying centered leads to integrity, why you sometimes need to step away from your day-to-day life to recenter yourself, and how sometimes you need to change something in your life to stay true to your center.*

My aikido academy attracted a lot of high-powered students in Washington, DC. I had State Department employees studying with me, FBI agents and CIA officers, U.S. and foreign diplomats, all sorts of people who were part of the country's—and the world's—power structure.

One of those students worked at the Russian embassy. And one day, some FBI agents approached me. It turned out that this Russian guy was a signals intelligence officer. His job was to intercept U.S. signals and try to crack our codes. In other words, the guy was a real-life spy. The FBI was pretty interested in getting close to him and keeping tabs on how his work was going, so they'd know if they needed to change their codes.

Except there was no way to get close to this guy. He was a total creature of habit. He lived at the embassy, he worked at the embassy. He didn't go out to restaurants or bars. He didn't date. He went to two places—the grocery store, and my aikido academy.

So the FBI had a proposition for me: They would place two undercover agents in the class with the Russian guy. These agents would use the opportunity of my class to try to befriend this guy, get close to him—do the whole spy thing. In return for my cooperation, they would be willing to fund a scholarship that would help some kid who otherwise couldn't afford it take classes at my school.

I had a choice to make: Should I let the agents infiltrate my class?

I am a Marine veteran. I volunteered to literally put my life on the line for my country. The idea of doing something to help the FBI appealed to my sense of patriotism. And let's face it, spy stuff is pretty cool. Having undercover FBI agents doing top-secret work in my school, with my help—it would be like living in a James Bond movie.

But helping these agents would mean lying to a student. And I would either have to lie to my staff or encourage them to lie. Was it worth it? What should I do? Which was more important—helping my country, or protecting my students?

We'll get to my decision in a minute. But first, in order to understand why I decided the way I did, it's essential to understand the Japanese concept of *nen*.

## FINDING YOUR CENTER OF GRAVITY

In aikido, we learn that it's crucially important to find what's called your *nen*. Nen literally means one-point, and it refers to your physical center of gravity, a point two inches below your navel. When you're fighting, if you find your one-point, it's much harder for your opponent to push you off balance. Metaphorically, nen refers to a line that connects your personal energy to the energy of the universe. It's the sense of cosmic balance that keeps you from being pushed over psychologically, by fear or overconfidence.

Finding your one-point is as crucial in life as it is in aikido. If you're not centered in yourself, any little thing can push you off balance. Picture yourself arriving at your office in the morning with one major item on your to-do list. You're focused, you're ready to tackle this project.

And then the e-mails start streaming in—your boss wants this assignment done by Friday. Now you're worried that you won't be able to finish in time. You're thinking about how much pressure your boss has been putting on you this year. Then you get another e-mail. Your colleague wants to get lunch, and you know what that means—an hour of listening to nonstop complaints. You can already feel the headache starting to throb behind your eyes. Next, it's your spouse texting to remind you to stop at the store on your way home, which is annoying, because you definitely weren't going to forget. Sure, you forgot yesterday, but today you've got a reminder on your phone. And so on. Before you know it, all that focus and purpose you walked in with is gone.

**The Mushin Way Peak Performance Tip**

Remove all "push" notifications from your electronic devices—no more automatic social media notifications, e-mail pings (you should have already removed e-mail from your device), and so on. Allowing push notifications is just asking to be interrupted.

That feeling of being buffeted from side to side by whatever's coming at you—that's the feeling of losing your one-point. It can happen on that kind of small scale, over the course of a day, and it can also happen on a larger scale, over the course of a year, or a lifetime. Your parents pressure you to go out for the soccer team because they think it'll look good on your college applications. You join a community choir to get closer to someone you find attractive. You take a job because you need a job, and then five years later you're stuck in a career you didn't particularly want.

Some outside influences are positive, of course. Some people encourage us to be our best, like the friend who makes a pact to go to the gym together once a week, or the spouse who always believes the best is possible. But all too often, we're influenced by other people's expectations in a way that really has nothing to do with what we really want. And because we want to please these people, or we fear letting them down, we let them push us in one direction or another. And we end up off-center. We lose our one-point.

## Staying Centered through Good Times and Bad

Investor Warren Buffett is famous for his low-key style. His annual letters to shareholders in his company, Berkshire Hathaway, are full of simple, down-to-earth advice, like: never overpay for an investment; always take a long-term view; never imagine that you can predict where the stock market is going next. Reading those letters, you'd think that being perhaps the world's most successful investor was just that simple. Buy good companies, at a discount if you can, and hold on to them for a long time. Apparently, that's all it takes to generate double the return of the S&P 500 over the course of 50 years.

And maybe it is—but it's sticking to that simple plan that's the hard part. Most people don't have the discipline to follow those simple rules in good times and in bad. They'll jump on the bandwagon of the latest shiny new IPO, and they'll overpay for that investment. They'll panic when the market starts to go south, and they'll forget their long-term view. They'll let ego or fear push them off their one-point, and they'll make a bad call.

Buffett has famously said he never invests in a company he doesn't understand. Often, that means that he favors businesses that continually, reliably produce cash, like insurance companies. It also means he tends to avoid jumping on the latest high-tech fad. That doesn't always make him popular. For example, in 1999, he gave a speech to a conference full of high-flying investors hyped on the dot-com boom—explaining why the boom wouldn't last. People dismissed him. He was right.

His personal style is just as simple and straightforward as his professional style. He favors burgers and fries, Heinz ketchup (he's an investor), root beer floats. For decades, he's kept his own salary steady at $100,000—a handsome sum, but nothing compared to the lavish salaries most CEOs enjoy.[1] He consistently gives credit to the colleagues at all levels of his business who have helped him achieve his enormous success. In his 2014 letter to investors, on the fiftieth anniversary of his taking over management of Berkshire Hathaway, he noted that investors attending the company's annual meeting could probably save some cash by flying into Kansas City instead of Omaha.[2] Think about that: This is a billionaire who still thinks about how to save a couple hundred dollars on a plane ticket.

Buffett's illustrious career is a great example of the power of holding to your one-point. He has said that you don't have to be a genius to be a successful investor; "what you need is the temperament to control the urges that get other people into trouble in investing."[3] What you need is nen: a psychological center of gravity that keeps you steady when the world around you is wavering. Listen to the way Buffett describes his life's work:

> I feel like I'm on my back, and there's the Sistine Chapel, and I'm painting away. I like it when people say, "Gee, that's a pretty good-looking painting." But it's my painting, and when somebody says, "Why don't you use more red instead of blue?" Good-bye. It's my painting.[4]

That is a perfect description of what it means to hold to your one-point. *It's my painting.* How often do you let yourself be swayed by someone else's opinion? How often do you pick up that red brush because of a comment, a suggestion, or a complaint?

## Give This a Try

If you are truly centered in your one-point, you can't be moved. There are a number of physical exercises we do in aikido classes to help students find their one-points. Here's a simple one that you can do with a partner: Have your partner push on your hips. If you're just standing however you would normally stand, they'll easily be able to knock you off balance. Try that and see how easy it is.

Next, get centered in your one-point and try it again. Bend one knee in front of you and keep your back leg straight, directing your energy through your extended leg into the ground. Lower your weight into your hips, sinking into your center of gravity, and then tilt your hips up. Then have your partner push on your hips again. If you're doing it right, they won't be able to move you. You'll be centered in your one-point, and they won't be able to knock you off balance.

As you're doing the exercise, you'll notice that it feels similar to the exercise we did in Chapter 2, on directing your ki in the right direction so that you can't be pulled off balance. Properly channeling your ki is an essential part of maintaining your one-point. Remember that when you're working on developing your ki, you need to focus on three things: (1) relaxing your body, (2) extending your limbs to direct your energy purposefully, and (3) finding your center of gravity to stay grounded. Ki and nen are two unique principles that when combined provide a solid physical and nonphysical foundation for success—in sports, life, and business.

Try this one-point exercise a few times until you can feel the difference between being centered and being off balance. Really focus on how your body feels when it's centered. Feel what it's like to have someone try to push you and to stay in your one-point. What would it be like to feel that unmovable, that steady, in your day-to-day life?

## FINDING YOUR ONE-POINT BY STEPPING AWAY

For years I put work ahead of everything else in my life. My twenties flew by while I was living, studying, and working in Japan. My thirties were a blur, moving back to America, starting and running successful companies. By age 42, I was completely burned out. I had achieved significant professional success. But I was lonely. And I'd never taken a two-week vacation in my life.

I know I'm not alone there. A recent survey by the executive search firm Korn/Ferry found that only 3 percent of executives across a range of industries were willing to completely cut themselves off from the office during vacation.[5] Why? What are we so afraid of? For me, I was afraid to delegate. I thought that only I could make all the necessary decisions and take care of all the important clients. So I kept pushing myself—until I finally hit the wall and I was no longer good to anyone: myself, my family, my friends, my staff, or my clients.

Finally, at age 42, I took a real vacation. For three weeks I traveled and rested and recharged. This was the first time in my life that I left my laptop at home and didn't look at e-mail, answer phone calls, or worry about work. I completely unplugged. My stress level dropped to near zero. I had fun, for the first time in many years.

That vacation showed me that my priorities were all wrong. I had put my own well-being way down on my list of priorities, behind my job, my family, my friends, and a host of other distractions. And the irony was, by not taking responsible care of myself and constantly putting my job at the top of the list, I was actually limiting my professional success.

When I finally stepped away, the disaster I was afraid of did not materialize. Quite the opposite, in fact. My staff thrived, my clients were exquisitely happy, important decisions were made with more creativity than I could have summoned—everything went great, and I came back refreshed and ready to work harder and smarter than before.

In Stephen Covey's bestselling book, *The Seven Habits of Highly Effective People*, he explains that one of the fundamentals of being productive is to take time off to rest. To exercise. To go on vacation. That time is not money. Because no matter how busy you think you are, if you don't take quality time off, you won't have the energy, creativity, and vigor to fulfill your other business and personal priorities in earnest. Your well-being cup will run dry.

So how do you keep your well-being cup full? Start slowly. Start by setting boundaries, such as staying off the Internet before 8:00 AM or after 7:00 PM. Stop working on the weekends. As I've been begging you to do throughout the book, remove wireless e-mail from your phone—trust me, you don't need it. And for your own sake and the sake of everyone around you, take a vacation. Sometimes you need to step away in order to recalibrate and find your one-point again.

## MAINTAIN YOUR ONE-POINT AND YOU'LL ACHIEVE INTEGRITY

Integrity has nothing to do with morality. I learned a great definition of integrity through a leadership development and executive coach training program I completed with Accomplishment Coaching[6] years ago: Integrity is about the alignment of three things—your intentions, your speech, and your actions. Maybe that's why it's so easy to love grifters and con men in movies like *Dirty Rotten Scoundrels*—they're honestly dishonest. Compare that to the heads of major banks who claimed to be responsible corporate citizens creating solid products and helping the economy, all while doing the exact opposite.

Finding and maintaining your one-point is the first step toward achieving integrity. For years, I stayed on in corporate America because I loved the excitement of making a big deal, and I liked raking in the big commissions they brought. But I wasn't in integrity. My intention has always been to make a positive difference in the world. I talked up those ideals all the time. But my actions weren't in alignment with my intentions and my speech. I wasn't in integrity.

For someone else, that job would have kept them in integrity. If I had been a person whose primary intention was to provide a good life for my family, then I would have been in perfect integrity by following through on that intention with my words and actions. But that wasn't me. Staying at that job was pulling me away from my one-point and pulling me out of integrity.

---

### The Mushin Way Peak Performance Tip

Change your work and cell voice mail to let the caller know you only check VM once or twice per day and, time permitting, will return calls later. Like e-mail, you don't have to be reactive and jump to listen to and return every voice mail and phone call. You are *not* that important, and people will quickly learn that you will call them back within 24 hours.

---

It's easy to tell when someone is out of integrity. You can sense it when you watch some politicians on TV (okay, a lot of politicians). You can feel it when you talk to a friend who's settling for the wrong job or the wrong relationship. You can definitely feel it in your gut when you're out of integrity. It's an uncomfortable feeling. We hate it when we see it in other people, and we hate it even more in ourselves.

Sometimes we hate it so much that we can't even admit to ourselves what's happened. When a reporter for *Stars and Stripes*, a military newspaper, revealed that NBC anchorman Brian Williams had exaggerated a story about being in a helicopter that took enemy fire, that was bad enough. He had strayed from his one-point and forgotten the most fundamental principle of his profession. But what was worse was how he responded to this scandal. He couldn't admit that he had lied.[7] In his on-air "apology," he said he "made a mistake in recalling the events of 12 years ago."

If you watched that apology, you felt that uncomfortable feeling we all get when we see someone who's out of alignment with themselves. Imagine if Williams had, instead, frankly apologized. What if he had said that his head got too big, he lied, and he was sorry? Wouldn't that have been more satisfying? Wouldn't that have ended the scandal much more quickly? Each time Williams told that exaggerated story, he was out of integrity. But if he had truly apologized, he would have brought himself back into integrity and returned to his one-point.

## Sometimes You Have to Make a Change to Remain Yourself

My consulting client Amanda came to me at a really difficult time in her life. She was a high-achieving professional who was not used to failing at anything. But she was going through a difficult divorce and struggling to keep her head above water at work while taking care of her 10-year-old daughter.

I encouraged her to leave her job and start her own consulting business. And I told her she should do it right away—even with everything else that was going on.

That may sound like crazy advice. But when I spoke to Amanda, I could see that part of the reason she was struggling was that she did not feel like she was leading the life she wanted or intended to live. Her divorce was, to some extent, out of her control—she could control her own behavior as she went through this difficult time, but she couldn't control her spouse's behavior, and she couldn't singlehandedly keep a marriage together. What she could control was her own work life, and that was out of balance.

Amanda was the kind of person who cares deeply about living a life that's aligned with her values. She felt uncomfortable working for whatever client came through the door—she wanted to be able to choose projects that she could feel fully engaged in and devoted to. Her current job wasn't giving her this kind of control. And feeling that lack of control in two such important areas of her life was pushing her dangerously far from her one-point.

As difficult as it was, leaving the security of that full-time job and beginning to work as a consultant was the perfect move for her at that moment. Setting up her own business allowed her to choose projects she was passionate about and felt authentically excited by. And it gave her the chance to take back her sense of control and autonomy, which was crucial to her well-being. Quitting her job and striking out on her own was the best way for her to take responsible care of herself.

It would have been easy for Amanda to let herself be pushed and pulled in all directions by the tumultuousness in her personal life. Between her divorce and her daughter, she certainly had plenty to worry about. And many people would feel that her highest priority at that moment should have been providing stability for her daughter. For some people in that situation, focusing on their child would have been the highest and best priority, and the best way to hold to their one-point.

> **The Mushin Way Peak Performance Tip**
>
> Reading fiction for as little as 6 minutes before going to sleep helps quiet and settle the mind. Read from a book and not an electronic device. The National Academy of Sciences found reading on a light-emitting device before bed (smartphone, tablet, e-reader, laptop, etc.) makes it more difficult to fall asleep, negatively impacts the quality of your sleep, and even adversely affects your performance the next day.

But not for Amanda. She was committed to living a life that matched her values, and she wasn't following through on that in her actions. She was off-center. And that off-centeredness was actually creating instability and conflict for her. When she left to start her own business, it was stressful, but it was a move that allowed her to live a more authentic life and hold on to her one-point. And that ultimately allowed her to be a better parent to her daughter.

For some of us, returning to one-point is simply a matter of reminding ourselves what our priorities and intentions are, and remembering to live intentionally to support those goals. It might be as simple as cutting back on TV in the evenings so you can spend more focused time with your spouse, friends, or family. Or maybe you need to set aside half an hour in the mornings to set goals for the day, so that you don't let e-mails and other interruptions keep you from moving your work forward.

But in some cases, finding your one-point may require a more radical change. If you're working at a job that pays the bills but doesn't align with your values; if you've settled for a relationship that lacks a true connection; if you're living halfway across the country from the family you claim is a top priority, it's time to take a clear look at where you are and where you need to be. Change can be scary, I know, but you will feel a deep sense of relief when you're able to align your actions with your intentions and return to your one-point.

## MICHAEL VELTRI, SUPER-SPY?

I felt that sense of deep relief when I said no to the FBI and told them they couldn't put undercover agents in my class. As cool and glamorous as an undercover operation sounded, I knew in my gut that it wasn't the right thing for me to do.

My intentions, and the messages I gave to my students, were all about helping my students make the impossible possible in their lives. I asked my students to trust me and allow me to help them reach their full potential. I told them I was 100 percent committed to them and to the work we did together. I couldn't then turn around and betray the trust of a student—not even for a good cause.

It would have been easy to let the idea of helping my country or the glamour of participating in this undercover sting pull me off my one-point and seduce me into betraying this core principle. But by maintaining my one-point, my focus, my grounding, my roots in what I truly believed, my healthy priorities, I was able to make a decision from an uncluttered mind. And I was able to make the decision that kept me in alignment with my deepest values—the decision that kept me grounded in my nen.

## The Mushin Way Action Step: How to Apply Nen—One-Point

Finding and holding to your one-point is all about knowing what your priorities are and acting accordingly.

Step 1: Start by listing the five to 10 top people, places, and pursuits where you currently spend the most time, energy, and focus. List them "as is"—not as you think they should be or want them to be. For example:

1. Work
2. Family
3. Friends
4. Clients
5. Customers

6. Sports
7. Church
8. Self
9. Volunteer commitments
10. Travel

Make your own "as is" list here (you don't have to fill in all 10, just as many as you can come up with):

1.
2.
3.
4.
5.

6.
7.
8.
9.
10.

Step 2: Next, reorganize your list to look the way you think it should. That is, in a perfect world, where would you like to spend most of your time, energy, and focus? What would come second? Third? And so on?

*(continued)*

(*continued*)

1.                                    6.

2.                                    7.

3.                                    8.

4.                                    9.

5.                                          10.

Step 3: Now move "Self" up to the top of the list, no matter what. If you do not focus your time and energy on responsible self-care, you will live your life from a weak and ineffective one-point. You must take great, responsible care of yourself to create a strong, stable one-point and ensure you are the best possible spouse, parent, employee, executive, business owner, friend, family member, servant leader, and the list goes on.

Step 4: Declare right now one thing you will do that will help you to *responsibly* take care of yourself so as to better serve the other people, organizations, and worthwhile causes in your life. Be specific. For example, "I will sign up for a new group exercise class that meets three times per week to help me lose 27 pounds so I will have more of the strength, vitality, and focus I need to succeed in my business and personal life."

My Responsible Self-Care Declaration is:

_____

_____

_____

*Do it. Now.*

Share your results with me, ask questions, get help, or post a comment for *The Mushin Way* community to read and respond at michaelveltri.com/book

# CHAPTER 5

# 無心 *Mushin: No-Mind/ No-Distractions/No-Fear*

*In this chapter, you will learn why bracing for attack is the best way to be beaten, and how letting go of expectation helps you react more quickly. You'll learn how meditation helps clear your mind to move into a space where you're reflecting the world around you instead of projecting your own fears and worries. You'll hear about some leaders who practice meditation, and you'll learn some simple ways to start learning how to clear your mind.*

The first time I threw a live hand grenade, I forgot what to do. I couldn't remember if it was "thumb clip, pull the pin," or "pull pin, thumb clip." And did I mention I was standing there holding a *live hand grenade*? It was a bad time to forget what to do.

I'm sure my Marine buddies were wondering why I was hesitating and what the hell I was doing. I'm sure they wanted to yell at me, too. But you're supposed to look away when something's about to explode, and these guys were doing exactly what they were supposed to do. They were looking away. I was the one with the problem.

I remember standing there with this live grenade in my hand, thinking, "The Marine recruiter really didn't tell me about this." He focused on the camaraderie of the Marine Corps, travel to exciting new places, the glamour of being part of one of the most elite fighting units in the armed forces. He didn't say anything about having to hold and throw live hand grenades.

Somehow I managed to rip the pin out, and it was "go-time." I couldn't put the pin back in. One wrong move and I'm dead.

I had three choices: One, make a good decision and throw it far enough that it wouldn't hurt anybody. Or two, make a bad decision and drop it, killing myself and my Marine buddies. Or worse yet, three—make no decision at all and hold onto that hand grenade. For the rest of my life.

## GIVE THE GRENADES TO THE ZEN MASTERS

You might think that what I needed most then was to remember the sequence. But aikido teaches us that what I actually needed to do was to clear my mind of everything, including the lecture I'd just listened to on the proper way to throw a damn hand grenade. I needed to stop thinking about that lecture, stop thinking about the Marines standing around me, stop thinking about looking "good" or "bad," stop thinking about whether I was about to make a truly stupid mistake. I needed to let go of my fear and ego and take relevant action. Quickly.

Imagine a student of classical swordsmanship who's just arrived at an isolated school, somewhere in the mountains of Japan, ready to spend several years studying and training. Imagine that this student is given only menial tasks to do, like washing the dishes and chopping the vegetables for dinner. He goes about his business, doing his best to complete his chores—but knowing all the while that, at any moment, his teacher could leap out of the bushes and hit him with a practice sword.

The great philosopher and student of Eastern traditions Alan Watts used this example in a lecture. He explained that pretty soon the fencing student is jumping at shadows, always braced for attack. The teacher is never where the student expects, attacking him at will. Finally the student gives up. There's no way to predict where this crazy teacher of his is going to pop up next. He relaxes. At that moment, Watts says, "He's ready to begin training."

When you're braced for attack, you're concentrating your energy in a particular direction. You think danger is lurking in that dark corner over there, so that's where you're concentrating all your senses. When the attack actually comes from the opposite direction, you're not ready, and that slows you down. It's only when you move into a state of no expectation, "no-mind," that you are ready to respond—in the moment—to the attack. It's only when you stop thinking about whether or not you're going to use the hand grenade properly that you can actually throw the damn thing away and save your own life.

## No Expectations, No-Mind

That state of no expectations—no distractions—is called *mushin* (pronounced "moo-sheen"). Literally, mushin means "no-mind" or "empty mind." But it doesn't mean not thinking. When you are in a state of mushin, your mind is like a mirror. As Watts explains in his lecture on the topic, "The mirror doesn't wait." It reflects what's happening around it instantly and perfectly. In a state of mushin, you have emptied your mind of distraction, anxiety, ego, fear—everything that holds you back and keeps you from seeing the truth of a situation. In a state of mushin, your mind is empty enough to receive that truth instantly, the way a mirror receives your reflection as soon as you step in front of it.

Mushin is not an absence of thought; it's a discipline that allows you to think spontaneously. When your mind is clear and calm, reflecting the world around you, you're not stuck hesitating and worrying about what to do. You think and act quickly because you're not distracted by extraneous thoughts. Mushin is about practicing this kind of deliberate spontaneity—not spontaneity in the shallow sense of being a "free spirit" who floats around avoiding responsibility, but a deeper, more meditative kind of spontaneity that comes from being fully present in the moment and responding to it thoughtfully and honestly, but with no hesitation.

> ### The Mushin Way Peak Performance Tip
>
> Set your desktop/laptop e-mail program (no wireless e-mail, remember) to manually pull in new messages. You don't want new messages automatically coming into your inbox every other second with their distracting chimes. Set it so you only see new e-mail when you purposefully check for new messages—and then set aside a time to do that, and only that, a couple of times a day.

As Watts explains, it can take years to learn to achieve a true state of mushin. At first, when you try to act spontaneously, you run the risk of doing something pretty stupid, because you're giving in to your first impulse, and we all have a lot of stupid impulses. But as you train and discipline yourself, you will gradually find that your spontaneous responses become more intelligent and appropriate. You will train yourself to think spontaneously. And you can start building this skill today.

Have you ever seen a great comedian respond to a comment from a heckler in the audience? There's no time to hesitate in that kind of moment. There's no time to stand there and think of the perfect comeback. And yet there are standup comedians out there who can, in an instant, produce that perfect comeback. I couldn't do that. You couldn't do that. Most of the time, when you or I open our mouths to make an off-the-cuff joke, it's pretty stupid. That's because we haven't spent time honing the craft of comedy. We haven't made hundreds and thousands of jokes and internalized what makes a joke land and what makes it fall flat. Paradoxically, effective spontaneity takes a lot of practice.

A comedian, a swordsman, or a CEO who makes that exquisitely perfect choice in an instant is able to do that because of practice—and because, in that moment, they've let all that practice go. It's become instinct. It exists somewhere outside of their conscious thought. In that moment of decision, their mind is empty. But that doesn't mean they're being thoughtless. It means they have achieved a state of mushin. It means their mind is like a clear mirror, reflecting the right action without hesitation.

## MINDFULNESS AND NO-MIND

So if it takes practice to develop a true, deep state of no-mind, what is that practice? Where do you start? These days, in the West, the ancient and powerful practice that helps you develop mushin is known as mindfulness.

Mindfulness, as it's practiced today in the West, is essentially a version of Zen meditation that's been stripped of much of its spiritual content. It's a relatively easy and accessible way for people to tap into the incredible power of this ancient discipline. There have now been dozens of studies that have confirmed what Zen and aikido masters have known for centuries—a regular meditation practice sharpens and clarifies the mind. It reduces stress.[1] Corporations around the world are starting to train their employees in mindfulness practice. Some researchers are even starting to see the benefit of not only training leaders in mindfulness but directly connecting that training to other coaching efforts.[2]

Leaders from all walks of life have spoken about how helpful the practice of mindfulness meditation has been in their work. Roger Berkowitz, the CEO of Legal Sea Foods, says he meditates twice a day.[3] It's the first thing he does every morning. "Sometimes," he says, "I'm wrestling with an issue before meditation, and afterward the answer is suddenly clear." That's a sign that Berkowitz is reaping the full benefit of meditation. When his mind is clear, when he's in a state of mushin, answers to difficult questions appear "suddenly." Meditation allows him to access this clear, reflective state of mind where he is able to think spontaneously.

Bill Ford, the executive chairman of Ford Motor Company, has described mindfulness as a lifeline that has helped him get through some of the biggest challenges in his life[4]—including the incredible challenge of the crisis of 2008, when he was forced to lay off thousands of people from a company he still views as a family business.[5] The people he had to fire were people he knew and who had known his family for generations. He has said that his meditation practice, and a simple practice of setting an intention of compassion for the day, helped him get through this incredibly difficult time.

Filmmaker David Lynch found transcendental meditation so emotionally transformative that he created the David Lynch Foundation for Consciousness-Based Education and World Peace in order to help more people learn about the practice.[6] In an interview with *The Seattle Times*, Lynch said that within two weeks of starting a meditation practice, his wife at the time noticed a drastic change—his anger and self-doubt had fallen away. Lynch said that many people experience a change in the way they think after they start meditating:

So something that people say is, "Before I started meditating, I just reacted. Now, with meditation, I have this pause and this reasoning: Do I really want to blow this man's head off with a .357 Magnum in my hand?" And then the answer is, "No, I don't think so." They have time to think.[7]

That's mushin. That's the spontaneous thinking that comes from true clarity. Without mushin, Lynch and others feel they have no time to think—they act out of an ignorant, impulsive form of spontaneity. When they find mushin, that split second when they need to make a decision expands. Suddenly, it feels like plenty of time because they're able to think spontaneously.

---

### Give This a Try

Starting a meditation practice may seem daunting. However, you can start practicing mindfulness in just a few minutes a day—and becoming more focused and less distracted by your hyperactive "monkey mind." Remember the meditation exercise you learned in Chapter 1? In case you don't, here is a reminder: Set aside 1 minute—perhaps just after you wake up, or after you have your first cup of coffee, or before you start or finish your workday. Sit in a quiet place. Turn off your phone. Shut out distractions. Sit up straight. Close your eyes slightly, but not all the way (you don't want to fall asleep). Take five slow, deep breaths. Breathe in and out slowly, counting each exhalation. When you find your mind beginning to wander—filling up with thoughts about your daily worries or joys—direct your attention back to counting your exhalation. It's that simple—and that difficult.

Now here is another easy practice you can try. It is called the "STOP" technique and is advocated by psychologist Elisha Goldstein and others.[8] This is a simple technique you can complete in 1 or 2 minutes and will help you calm

*(continued)*

(*continued*)

and empty your mind. It's organized around the acronym STOP: First, you *Stop* what you're doing; then you *Take* a few deep breaths; then you *Observe* how your body feels in the moment; then you *Perceive* sounds in the room around you. This is another simple way to start letting go of anxious, worried thoughts and to start moving into a state of mushin.

## EMPTYING YOUR MIND ISN'T EASY

Starting a meditation practice doesn't take that much time—but that doesn't mean it's easy. Especially for an extrovert like me. One of the hardest things I've ever done is go on a weeklong meditation retreat at a Zen monastery in Japan. And remember, I've gone through Marine Corps boot camp and intensive chemotherapy almost daily for three months.

I like to work hard. I'm good at working hard. But learning to meditate isn't the kind of thing that responds to hard work in the traditional sense. Meditation is an elusive practice—all you can do is put in the time. It takes incredible discipline—but paradoxically, trying harder may only put you further away from your goal.

Learning to meditate, for me, was an experience unlike any other. On this meditation retreat, I was surrounded by people. At any one time there were between 10 and 30 people around, working, sleeping, and meditating. I love being part of a group—as an extrovert, I'm a team player—but this was a group existing in total silence. I was surrounded by people, but I was completely alone inside my own head. In a world that can't stop talking and communicating, I was forced to be quiet. Not only to stop talking, but to quiet my mind.

## SILENCING THE MONKEY MIND

When you sit down to meditate, what Zen masters call the "monkey mind" starts running around. The monkey mind is that anxious, jumpy, excitable, angry, frightened creature that lives inside all of us. And when you stop talking and settle into silence, that's all you can hear—your own fear and anger, your worries, your ego. Your own internal monkey, swinging around, screaming, causing all sorts of trouble.

During the weeklong meditation retreat, physically, we were all sore, because you're sitting still for such a long time. As a lifelong athlete, I'm used to being sore—but I'm used to pushing my body to do something, and I found that forcing my body to do nothing was much more difficult. You're sitting there, and you're sore, and you have nothing else to think about. All you can do is focus on how sore you are, and that only amplifies the soreness. Time seems to stop. You think it's been 45 minutes and you're almost done, and you look at a clock, and it's only been 2 minutes. It's an unbelievable challenge on every level—physically, mentally, emotionally.

At the end of the first day of that retreat, I remember thinking to myself, *My God, I have to do this for another six days? I can't believe I agreed to do this. There's no way I'm going to get through this.*

---

**The Mushin Way Peak Performance Tip**

When speaking or writing, replace the word "but" with "and" or, at the very least, "however." This creates a positive subconscious connection with whomever you're communicating with—even if you have to deliver bad news. Try it and see.

When you're meditating, you're overwhelmed by silence. You've got nowhere to go but your own mind. You have to face your fear, your ego, your doubt. Left to the solitude of your own thoughts, you can either become your own best ally or your own worst enemy. You can't push through it—there is no "through" to push. There is only this moment, and then the next moment, and then the next. The second you think that you're making progress, you're no longer meditating—you're thinking about meditating. And the second you think that you're not making progress, you're also not meditating, you're thinking about meditating. There goes that monkey swinging on by. Troublesome little bugger.

Learning how to meditate is one of the most difficult things you will ever do because it requires you to accept parts of yourself you normally don't want to face. In the silence of your own mind, all the parts of yourself you like the least will become crystal clear. And you have to be with it all—the good, the bad, and the ugly—in silence. For many of us, confronting the insides of our own minds is the hardest thing we'll ever have to do.

## THE OPPOSITE OF MUSHIN

For most of us, most days, the insides of our minds are chaos. We're thinking a thousand thoughts a minute. We're constantly distracted. Our attention is constantly being pulled in all sorts of different directions by our smartphones and our laptops. The second we start to focus our thoughts, there's a ping pulling us back in the other direction—an e-mail from a coworker, a text from a friend, another comment on Facebook. . . .

No wonder so many of us have trouble making decisions. Say you need a new smartphone. Your old one is a few years old, and the battery runs down really quickly. So you go online to buy a new one. Simple, right? In a couple of clicks, you can have some robots in a warehouse somewhere picking up your new smartphone and sending it your way. Except—an hour after you've picked up your laptop, you've read about 107 reviews of a whole bunch of different phones, you've read three different articles about iOS versus Android, and you're deep into a text-message conversation about which of seven different movies to watch tonight.

Sound familiar? Our world today is designed to provide us endless options, but it is definitely not set up to create clarity. In fact, the more options we have, the more we struggle to make a choice. The more decisions we have to make, the more difficult it is to make each decision. Psychologists call this decision fatigue,[9] and they've found that decisions involving trade-offs—the cheapest smartphone or the one with the best camera?—are particularly tiring. That means the more complicated a decision is, the more difficult it is to make—and after you make it, you're going to have an even harder time making the next decision.

## A Better Way to Make Decisions

Maybe one of the reasons we struggle to make effective decisions is that we go about it wrong. We don't understand how we really should be making decisions. We think the best way to approach that new smartphone problem is to analyze the question from every angle and look at the pros and cons of all the different options. But in reality, decision making is not an entirely rational process.

Neurologist Antonio Damasio had a patient named Elliot who had a brain tumor.[10] After treatment, he had lost some of the portion of his brain that was responsible for allowing him to feel emotions—and he was incapable of making a simple decision. He could spend all day debating how to organize a set of files—alphabetically? By topic? By date?

Damasio concluded that emotions are necessary to the decision-making process. He argued that something he called a "prehunch," a subconscious, almost instinctual reaction to a problem, is essential in making good decisions. Later experiments proved that people with damage to the emotional centers of their brains were much slower than undamaged subjects to recognize when a card game was rigged against them. For subjects with normal, undamaged brains, their emotional, instinctual brains tipped them off to the unfairness of the game long before their rational brains had been able to analyze the situation. They had a "prehunch." The subjects whose emotional brains were damaged didn't get hunches. They only had their slow-moving rational brains to rely on.

> ### The Mushin Way Peak Performance Tip
>
> For an optimum night's sleep, and thus, optimum next-day performance, you can "go vampire"—ensure your bedroom is cool, dark, and quiet. Coffin optional. And totally not recommended. . . .

Trying to make a good decision with your slow-moving rational brain is never going to work. It'll lead you down that rabbit hole of endless smartphone reviews. It'll lead you to analysis paralysis. I once hired a general manager who was a brilliant guy, but he suffered terribly from analysis paralysis. He was a great planner. He could make these exquisite, detailed, long-term project plans—but he couldn't take the first step to put it into action. Step one could be something as simple as "decide who on our staff should be on the project team," and he'd be stuck on step one for days. This guy was smart. He was a hard worker, and he meant well. But he was stuck. Eventually, I had to fire him—it was heart-breaking to let him go, but he just couldn't get anything done.

Don't get me wrong—making decisions in the mushin way doesn't mean making dumb decisions. It doesn't mean you don't think through your options. But it does mean you don't let those options paralyze you. You analyze and think through the problem, and then you take a moment to clear your head. You empty your mind of all the thoughts and worries clouding it, and you look for that little voice inside you that already knows what to do. You listen for that "prehunch" that comes from somewhere much deeper than your rational brain. And then you take action.

What my poor paralyzed general manager couldn't see was that his desire to find the perfect answer was holding him back from taking action. Ultimately, done is better than perfect. Done is the bridge that leads you to your next phase of growth. An imperfect step forward is at least a step in the right direction.

Moving into a state of mushin helps you get unstuck and move into relevant action. It's an exercise in letting go of your ego. The ego tells you that you have to be perfect. That if you don't get it exactly right, people will reject you. Fear tells you that you will fail. That you aren't capable of moving forward. That you don't have what it takes. In order to move forward, you have to let go of your ego and your fear, clear your mind—and decide. Move. Take action. Now.

## The *Mushin* Way Action Step: How to Apply Mushin—No-Mind/No-Distractions/No-Fear

The great irony is, wanting to practice mushin is actually counter to the concept of mushin. That is, if you want to practice mushin, you're already not being spontaneous. You're trying to force spontaneity, which is impossible.

*(continued)*

(*continued*)

So how can you practice mushin and still embrace its true essence? To get closer to mushin, you must chisel away at the many distractions that bombard you in your business and personal life, stealing your focus and dividing your attention. Here is one simple exercise that proves how choosing to focus on one—and only one—task at a time, and seeing it all the way through to completion, actually makes you *more* productive and produces higher-quality work than trying to "multitask."

### "Multitasking Is a Myth" Exercise

Step 1: In the space below, I want you to write out the phrase, "Multitasking is a myth."—while multitasking! Write one letter of the phrase and a sequential number underneath it. So you'll write "M" and then the number "1" directly underneath it; then "U" and "2," and so on—letter, then number. Letter, then number. Be sure to also put a number underneath the spaces and punctuation mark. Time how long it takes you to do this from start to finish:

M U L . . .

1   2   3

Time to Complete: _____

Step 2: Now do the same exercise *without* multitasking. See each specific task through to completion: (1) Write out—print or cursive—the entire phrase "Multitasking is a myth." (2) After writing the phrase, number the letters, spaces, and punctuation underneath from 1–23.

Step 1: Multitasking is a myth.

Step 2: 1 2 3 4 . . . 22 23

Time to Complete: _____

Step 3: Compare the two times. The second, non–multitasking time, should be much faster than the first. Look at Step 1, when you multitasked. Did you spell the phrase correctly? Some will have misspelled the phrase or forgotten some of the letters. How many numbers do you have? Some people will have fewer than 23 and some people will have more than 23. Some people will have forgotten to number the spaces and punctuation mark.

Not only does multitasking take way longer, it produces inferior results. *The Mushin Way* is about being present and seeing one, and only one, task through to completion before moving on to the next.

Step 4: Practice. Without multitasking, make one phone call—to your parents, spouse, siblings, or best friend. Tell them something nice you like about them, because, why not? If they don't pick up, leave them the coolest voice message they ever got from you. *Do it. Now.*

You are halfway through the book—great job! You've learned many helpful concepts, principles, tools, and techniques. Using what you've learned so far, try this:

## Get Into Action, Now

1. Pick another decision or project you've been putting off— or keep working on one goal or project you chose in an

*(continued)*

*(continued)*

earlier chapter. Perhaps you want to change jobs, buy that dream house, or move to a new city. Have you been putting off having a tough conversation with your spouse, parents, siblings, boss, or colleagues? Write it below:

_____

_____

_____

2. Clearly identify what you want to gain for yourself by completing this goal. Now, pick a date when you will have it completed. Remember, this *must* be a goal that inspires you and you want to do because you see the benefit for yourself. If you are trying to accomplish something from guilt, obligation, force, or from a sense of duty, you either won't complete it, or you'll produce a mediocre result, at best.

   For example: I want to increase my monthly take-home income by $2,500 in after-tax dollars so I can pay down my student loans and put the rest away into savings. I want to produce this additional $2,500 net income per month within 120 days.

   Write your guilt-free, inspiring goal here:

_____

_____

_____

3. Remember, you cannot succeed by yourself. Reference the list of family members, mentors, friends, colleagues, and consultants you identified in Chapter 2. *Without* multi-tasking, get into relevant action and build your team. Remember, when you ask for help from your team, you have to show them how *they* will benefit from helping you

accomplish your goal. Write down one and only one relevant action step you can complete within 30 minutes that will help you move closer to completing the goal you declared above:

My relevant action step that can be completed in 30-minutes or less is:

_____

_____

_____

*Do it. Now.*

When you get stuck—and you will—let me know how I can help you get unstuck by leaving a comment at michaelveltri.com/book. Also be sure to let me know what's working for you, what new ideas you've come up with, and share your wins with *The Mushin Way* community.

# CHAPTER 6

## 入り身 *Irimi: To Enter*

*In this chapter, you will learn why it's so important to strike directly at the core of a difficult problem. You'll hear about how aikido is based on centripetal force and requires practitioners to get close to their opponents, and you'll learn what can happen when you fail to get close to the heart of a problem. You'll learn how to tell the heart of a problem from a distracting tangent, and you'll learn how to confront the problem of distraction in your own life.*

The toughest aikido class I ever taught was a bunch of teenage girls. I'd been brought in to teach aikido at one of the most exclusive, private, all-girl high schools in Washington, DC. The girls in this school were straight out of the movie *Mean Girls*— privileged, entitled, ruling their own corner of the world.

I'm used to teaching high-achieving adults. In most of my classes, my students want to be there and are excited to learn. We tend to share a similar outlook on life. This class was different. This was a room full of teenage girls, ages 15 to 18, who were basically there just to get gym credit. This was a completely different challenge, and I wasn't prepared for it.

As a teacher, I am patient and encouraging, even as I set high standards and expect my students to exceed them. With highly motivated adults, this attitude works fine. With these high school students, it was a disaster. To them, my friendly demeanor came across as weakness, and they took full advantage of it. Almost from the minute I walked in the door, I had lost them. Soon, these girls were showing up in inappropriate outfits, talking on their cell phones during class, and worst of all, horsing around, trying out dangerous aikido moves on their friends and worse yet—their *frenemies*. The aikido techniques I teach are dangerous if you don't know what you're doing. These kids were going to hurt themselves if I didn't do something.

> ### Mushin Way Peak Performance Tip
>
> Most of us check our e-mail first thing in the morning. Don't. You're letting other people set your agenda for the day. Do your high-priority work first, and then check e-mail when you are ready to take a mental break.

I needed to take action, and I needed to do it fast. The heart of the problem was that I hadn't established my own authority strongly enough from the start. I could have tried to become a Marine drill instructor overnight, but I knew that wouldn't ring true to them. Changing my behavior would have been a distraction from the central issue: I had lost my credibility as an authority figure. And the class needed strong, central, and immediate authority.

So I brought in two female black belts from my aikido academy to be that authority. These women knew the techniques we needed to teach perfectly, and more important, they were fresh faces. Briefed by me on the situation, they walked in and, from minute one, established that they were in charge.

The second year I taught at this school, I had learned my lesson. I established myself as the authority from minute one, and I didn't have any more problems. But I wouldn't have gotten a second chance at that school if I didn't confront the problem directly and immediately. That is *irimi*—immediately entering to the heart of the problem to successfully solve it.

## CENTRIPETAL FORCE—YOU HAVE TO GET CLOSE

Aikido requires practitioners to do something very difficult. At the moment when a fight is beginning, you are asked to move toward your attacker—not away. This is one of the core principles of aikido. In Japanese, it's called *irimi* (pronounced "eerie-me"), which literally means "to enter." Aikido is based on centripetal force. It's a grappling art, and as in all grappling arts, including wrestling, Brazilian jujitsu, and judo, to execute any of the techniques properly, you have to get close enough to your opponent to touch them.

Aikido is known as the martial art of peace. But that doesn't mean the goal is to avoid conflict—quite the contrary. When you are challenged, you are asked to move closer to that challenge, to confront the problem directly. Even if you're facing a stronger, larger opponent, you're asked to move in, to get close, to enter.

This focus on entering directly into conflict doesn't mean you are meeting your opponent's forceful attack with force. Your goal is still to blend with their energy and redirect it. But you can't do that from a distance. You have to get in close. Imagine you're facing a big opponent who's squared off, ready to punch you. When his arm moves, all his energy is directed outward. If you get closer to him, you will actually be safer, because you'll be inside the range of his arm where there is less power and force. And once you have gotten close to him, you'll be able to execute another move designed to redirect his energy.

This is exactly what I did with those girls in my high school aikido class. They were testing my authority and pushing aggression to the limit. I could have tried to make myself into a wall they could bounce off—but instead, I moved closer to the problem and redirected their energy.

### Give This a Try

You can easily practice this principle physically in your day-to-day life. In Chapter 4, we discussed the concept of nen—maintaining one-point. Physically, maintaining one-point means keeping a low, balanced center of gravity. This simple exercise will allow you to practice maintaining one-point while also practicing irimi, or entering.

The next time you're walking through a crowded area like a mall, a subway or train station, an airport, or your busy workplace, think about keeping a low center of gravity. Keep your knees slightly bent, let your arms hang loosely by your sides, and take big, deep belly breaths. This will help keep you ready to move quickly.

Now, as you're walking, try not to radically change directions if you see people coming straight at you or space narrowing around you. Instead, maintain your one-point and turn a shoulder forward to slip past the people—close, but without bumping into them—like two ships passing closely in the night. This is irimi, entering—you're getting closer to the problem instead of trying to avoid it.

Keep your arms close by your sides and "glide" in and out of the crowded area, trying not to make contact with anyone. Don't stare at one person or group of people. Gaze into the distance and let your peripheral vision show your mind's eye what is coming at you, next to you, and even behind you. Keep track of how many times you bump into or make contact with someone. The more you practice entering and moving through a crowd, the less contact you will make and the more efficiently you will find yourself moving—much more efficiently than if you kept changing direction all the time.

When you're walking down a crowded sidewalk, you have to have some reaction to a person who's walking right at you. But in life, it's all too easy to avoid directly confronting a problem. You're swamped with work, but you don't want to admit it, so you stretch yourself to the breaking point to get everything done instead of going to your boss and telling her you've overburdened. Your relationship has hit the rocks, but the holidays are coming up, so you put off doing anything about it for a while. Your neighbor is driving you crazy playing loud music late at night, but instead of talking to him directly about it, you leave a passive-aggressive note.

As easy as it is to avoid direct confrontation, it's also easy to confront the wrong part of a problem. Instead of talking to your boss about your workload, you snap at your colleague who didn't finish his part of the project. Instead of having a real talk about the health of your relationship, you snap at your spouse for leaving dirty dishes in the sink. Maybe you call the cops on your neighbor and make a noise complaint. You take action—you force a confrontation—but it's the wrong action in response to the wrong problem. It's a distraction from the heart of the issue.

Aikido shows us a more elegant path. This path requires courage. It's the emotional equivalent of moving in close to execute a self-defense technique on the huge opponent who's attacking you. But it's the only way to actually solve a problem—move closer. Get to the heart of the matter. Enter.

## Not Confronting a Problem Can Be Disastrous

Kodak provides a classic example of a business that failed to practice irimi. The company's failure to capture the opportunity provided by digital technology is infamous. In 2012, Kodak filed for bankruptcy protection and has since essentially exited the consumer camera market. That's a huge fall from grace for a company whose name was for decades synonymous with the idea of snapshots. The "Kodak moment" is a thing of the past.

Kodak had every opportunity to become a leader in digital photography. The digital camera was literally invented at Kodak, by one of their employees.[1] Steven Sasson, the engineer who created the first digital camera, has said he was told by management, "That's cute—but don't tell anyone about it."

The story gets worse. In 1981, Sony brought out the first consumer digital camera. So Kodak commissioned research into this new phenomenon.[2] They wanted to know whether this digital thing was going to catch on, and how quickly. The answers that came back were almost eerily accurate: yes, and in about 10 years.

So what did Kodak do next? They worked on digital technology—and used it to build a film camera with a digital view screen on the back. The wrongheadedness here is almost funny until you remember all the people who lost their jobs because of this company's obstinate refusal to confront this existential threat to their business. This company literally invented the digital camera and then left it on a shelf for decades. They were told how long they had to solve the problem, and they did nothing.

## The Real Cost of Avoiding a Problem

Confronting problems is painful and difficult, so we put it off. It's human nature. But as Kodak's story proves, that desire to avoid confrontation is a potentially fatal flaw. When Steven Sasson built that first digital camera, it sounds like Kodak managers knew exactly what they were looking at. "Don't tell anyone about it" was the response. In other words, this thing could kill our comfortable film-based business. So let's not talk about it. Let's sweep it under the rug. Let's pretend it never happened.

How often have you done that in your work or personal life? You hear that your company's quarterly results weren't great and layoffs are probably coming—and you sit tight and hope for the best. A customer explains exactly why they're switching to another vendor, but you don't tell your boss because the big rebranding project was his baby, and he's not going to like hearing that it didn't work. So you sit tight and hope the next meeting goes better. Your wife mentions wanting kids, and you've never wanted kids, but you don't say anything because—well, people can change their minds, right?

### The Mushin Way Peak Performance Tip

Ensure all e-devices (laptop, smartphone, tablet, etc.) are wirelessly "push-synched." That is, any changes and edits to e-mail, calendar items, contacts, notes, documents, and so on automatically and instantly synchronize across all of your devices. For more info on how to do this, check out my website at michaelveltri.com/book

In 1981, when that research project gave them a clear deadline, Kodak could have sprung into action to get ahead of the trend and deliver a consumer-ready digital camera in 10 years or less. Instead, they reacted like so many of us do when we're given a timeline for a difficult or unpleasant task: They put off dealing with the problem. *Ten years is a long time*, you can imagine them thinking. *We can sell a lot of film-based products between now and then.*

## PROCRASTINATORS, TAKE NOTICE!

Avoiding confrontation is one way we fail to practice irimi; procrastinating is another. Every time you put off that tough phone call, watch another episode of your favorite show instead of working on that application that's not due for another two months, or decide you'll stick it out at your dead-end job just until after the holidays, you fail to practice irimi. And the funny thing is, you know it. Procrastinators don't feel good about procrastinating. They are constantly living under the shadow of that problem they're putting off. They are thinking about that problem all the time. Procrastinating only increases their stress.

So why do we do it? Because irimi takes real courage. It would have taken real courage for a Kodak manager to be the one to stand up and say, "We all know we can't keep doing this film thing forever." It takes courage to have that hard conversation. It takes courage to put yourself out there and apply for the job, fellowship, or grad program you've got your eye on. But summoning that courage and confronting the problem is the only way to succeed. It's the same kind of courage a student of aikido must summon in order to move closer to their opponent at a moment when they're under threat.

When they finally did start to develop digital technology, Kodak exhibited a third common failure to practice irimi: They took action, but not the kind of relevant action that would have taken them closer to the center of the problem. They brought out a camera with digital elements—that beautiful digital display on the back that let you preview your picture—but they didn't develop a digital camera. They were still wedded to film. And that left them with a product that didn't really make any sense.

In aikido, irimi means physically getting in close to your opponent's body. When a big brute is attacking you, you ignore the way he's swinging his arms and you move in close, going straight for his center of gravity. In business and in life, irimi means getting at the heart of the problem. Taking action on a tangential or related matter may make you feel like you're making progress, but in many cases it's really only holding you back. Building that half-digital camera held Kodak back from confronting the heart of the problem of digital technology, just the way that tidying your desk because you can't work in a messy environment can hold you back from actually doing your work.

## How to Tell the True Problem from a Distracting Tangent

Sometimes finding the heart of a problem is easy. If the problem is a disagreement with someone, you've got to talk to them. But not every problem is so clear-cut. Kodak's problem is staggeringly obvious in retrospect, but if you put yourself in the shoes of a Kodak manager in 1989, you can imagine how it might have looked more complicated. Yes, digital technology is on its way, and yes, history only moves in one direction. But your whole business is built around film and printing. That's what you know how to do. That's what you pay your employees to do. Surely there's still going to be a use for those people and that know-how. Surely your whole conception of your business doesn't have to change.

Of course, that business did have to change. But from the perspective of a person in the middle of that situation, with all the fears and attachments that they've accumulated over the course of their career, it was confusing enough to put off taking action or to attack the wrong part of the problem.

So how do you find the heart of a complicated problem? Once you've summoned the courage to take action, how do you know the relevant action to take?

You have all the knowledge you need—you just need to free yourself to find it. You can do this by using some of the techniques we've discussed in previous chapters, such as meditating, summoning calm energy, and getting your "top 5 team" to help you. Your team can help you find the relevant course of action that you can't see because it's stuck in your blind spot. We need other people we trust to help us break through our resistance—our fear, ego, guilt, obligation—and enter close to the problem to see the solution we can't see.

Often, if you take a moment to clear your mind and sit still for a while, your subconscious will take over, do its job, and the right action will come to you. That's how the phrase "let me sleep on it" came about. When you sleep, your subconscious works wonders and often produces the right solution for you.

## Confronting the Smartphone Problem

In 2010, I decided to remove e-mail from my smartphone. This was a huge step for me. I was as chained as anyone could be to that thing. I was looking at it from morning until night. Here was my morning routine for years; see if this sounds familiar. My iPhone alarm goes off, I reach over to turn it off and immediately start looking at work e-mails, text messages, social media posts, and a million other alerts that have popped up overnight. My heart rate increases, my stress levels spike, and my mind is polluted with worry about all the things I have to do. I quickly jump in the shower and eat breakfast (sometimes) and rush to get in front of my laptop. Then it's off to the races—a hamster on a wheel—spinning, running, working. Going nowhere. Getting nothing accomplished. Pretty soon, more panic would set in.

> **The Mushin Way Peak Performance Tip**
>
> Another health benefit of drinking green tea—your brain thinks you ate more when you consume a cup after a meal. Try drinking a cup of green tea after lunch and/or a cup of decaf green tea after dinner.

We live in a hyperconnected, 24/7/365, information-overloaded, distracted world. Can you believe that a recent study shows that we look at our smartphones, on average, 110 times per day?[3] Some users look at their phone a whopping 1,000 or more times per day. Sixty percent of adult professionals with a smartphone are connected to work 13.5 hours per day—texting, e-mailing, talking, exchanging voice mail, using other specialized work apps.[4] That is a 72-hour work week, at least. This leads to very little presence. Very little joy. No time off.

We're all aware of how corrosive the constant beeps and pings from our smartphones are to the quality of our attention and our ability to get real work done. We know these things stress us out. We know we can't do our best work for 13.5 hours a day. We moan and groan when we get that e-mail from the boss at 7 PM on Sunday night—and then we respond to it. We hate it when someone else is constantly checking their phone while we're talking to them, but we do it when they're talking.

Finally, in 2010, I decided I had had enough. It was time to practice irimi and confront this problem directly. Of course, living in this always-on, hyperconnected, demanding world of work is a huge problem, and there were a lot of steps I had to take to fully solve that problem and clear the mental and emotional space for me to do my best work. Faced with that huge problem, removing wireless e-mail from my phone might seem like a tangent or distraction. Wouldn't irimi require me to go straight to—well, changing my entire life to create an atmosphere of focus?

In this case, having e-mail on my smartphone was a small piece of a larger problem—but it was a part of the core of the problem, which was my attention was stretched too thin and I was trying to do too much. Removing e-mail from my phone was a step toward the core of the problem. It was an important step. And it produced immediate results.

## STARTING SMALL IS STILL STARTING

I remember a time before my e-mail purge when I was meeting with a client in my office. I was sitting across from this person trying to have a conversation—while looking at e-mail on my laptop. And also reading and answering a text that had just arrived.

Have you ever done that to someone? Or have you ever been the client in that situation and had some overdistracted vendor, boss, employee, husband, wife, friend, or child do the same to you? How did it feel? Pretty terrible, right? And what do you think happened to that client who sat in front of me while I was overly distracted? Yeah. He is no longer my client.

I've talked to a lot of people about this decision to remove wireless e-mail from my phone, and I hear the same reactions over and over: *I could never do that* or *I wish I could, but my boss/spouse would never go for it.* Well, I'm here to tell you that you can do it, and people will adjust. If it worries you, add a signature line to your e-mail that says something like, "I check e-mail three times a day during the workday. I will respond to your message as soon as I can." And then stick to that plan. You'll be surprised how quickly people around you will get used to your new system. In fact, I'm pretty sure you'll find that people prefer the new, less distracted you.

When you remove the distraction of e-mail from your phone, you are starting to take back control. You are practicing irimi and maintaining your center, creating balance, harmony, and focus. Once you stop being reactive to inbound distractions such as e-mails, text messages, and social media posts, you can start to batch your time into focused, undisturbed periods of work.

Remember, "time management" is a myth—you cannot manage time. You can, however, manage your energy and focus. You can't solve the whole problem of the twenty-first century world of distraction at once, but you can take concrete, decisive action that will make an immediate difference in your own stress levels and the quality of your professional and personal relationships. That's irimi, and I promise you, if you do it, you will immediately feel how powerful confronting a problem can be.

## THE POWER OF IRIMI

My consulting client Tom came to me with a huge problem. He was a manager at a global corporation, and his team worked out of several offices around the world. His direct reports were mostly engineers, and they weren't necessarily natural team players. These were people who liked to and were used to doing things their own way and solving problems on their own. He was really struggling to create a cohesive team out of this far-flung group.

As if that weren't tough enough, there was one very successful, big-ego player on the team, Evan, who was a real pain. He was constantly causing friction in the group because he was curt, even rude, with his teammates. He couldn't take advice or suggestions from anyone else. Given that the team was already struggling to work together, he was very clearly holding them back.

I coached Tom to confront the problem directly. He had spent months talking one-on-one to people, including Evan, trying to get them to be more cooperative and collaborative. He had talked to Evan multiple times about his attitude. But he hadn't been practicing irimi. He had been holding this problem at arm's length instead of entering on it and taking decisive action.

Tom and I worked together to come up with a plan. First, he needed to confront the problem of Evan. In the past, he had tried to nudge or encourage or even ask Evan to change his behavior. He'd talked to other people about how difficult Evan was and tried to help them come up with strategies for how to deal with him better. Now, with my support, he sat Evan down and gave him an ultimatum: He would have to change his attitude, or he was out. Fired. Gone. Sayonara.

That conversation was a huge step forward. Tom had practiced irimi by confronting a piece—a crucial piece—of the core problem of his disconnected team. Now he needed to keep going and get even closer to the heart of the problem. We worked together to design a training program for his team, and then he had them all fly in for two days of collaborative learning.

This training made a huge difference for the team. It brought them together so they could start to make personal connections with one another. And it gave Tom the opportunity to share his vision for the team's work, so they could see why he was prioritizing this project over that or asking them to do things in a certain way. Practicing irimi made a huge difference in helping Tom to transform this far-flung group of individuals into a true team.

You can circle a problem and learn about it and research and observe forever, but at some point, you have to enter and take relevant action. Aikido teaches us not to fear our fears, to solve our problems by confronting them directly and going straight to the heart of things. That's irimi, and it's incredibly powerful.

## The Mushin Way Action Step: How to Apply Irimi—To Enter

The concept of irimi shows us how entering directly to the center of a problem will help us take more relevant action more quickly.

**Step 1.** Irimi helps us cut through the clutter and confusion that prevents us from achieving peak performance, balance, and success. Answer the following with the first thing that comes to mind—"I would have more joy, prosperity, and success in my life if . . ."

_____

_____

_____

**Step 2.** Restate what you wrote above as a positive, specific, and achievable *declaration*. For example, if you answered the question above as, "I would have more joy, prosperity, and success in my life if I made more money at work," rewrite it as, "I will increase my salary by 25 percent six months from today."

My specific declaration is:

_____

_____

_____

**Step 3.** Now, enter—irimi. What is one simple action step you can complete in 30 minutes or less to move your declared goal forward?

*(continued)*

(*continued*)

My simple action step to complete in 30 minutes or less is:

_____

_____

_____

**Step 4.** Use the tools, techniques, and tips you've learned from the book and get into relevant action. Right now, no matter what time it is—*go. Do it.* You'll be one step closer to more joy, prosperity, and success.

Leave a comment or post a question on my website for help, ideas, and encouragement. Or just let me know what you accomplished by referencing this Chapter 6 exercise at michaelveltri.com/book

# CHAPTER 7

## 呼吸 *Kokyu: Breath-Power*

*In this chapter, you will learn how surviving cancer taught me a new awareness of the power of each breath. You'll hear about an exercise I use in my aikido classes to teach students to use their natural breath-power, and you'll learn why that exercise also teaches students to let go of their ego and stay focused. You'll encounter some strategies for learning how to harness and control your breath power in stressful situations and in day-to-day life. You'll learn how and why to take exhale moments that will help you let go of ego and fear in order to make better decisions and reach peak performance.*

I lost half of a lung to cancer. I'd been through treatment already for testicular cancer. Then the cancer spread to my lungs, so I'd gone through months of exhausting, debilitating chemotherapy. Then, after all that, there was still a spot on my lung. The doctors said it could be scar tissue left over from the brutal chemotherapy, but I didn't want to take any chances. I chose to have surgery to be sure.

I still remember waking up after that surgery with all these tubes coming out of me. For 24 hours after surgery, I was on a ventilator. A machine was breathing for me. Gradually, they weaned me off the ventilator. I had to learn how to breathe again—with half of one lung missing. Normally, we don't use our full body to breathe. We use our lungs. We don't use our full capacity. But I had to learn to breathe in with my whole body. Otherwise, I would constantly be taking these shallow breaths.

For a while, I felt like I was always out of breath. I tired easily. Suddenly, I knew exactly what oxygen was doing for my body. I knew, on this completely visceral level, the power each breath gave me. If you've ever traveled to a place that's at a very high elevation, you may have some idea of what I'm talking about—it's not until you take in a little less oxygen with each breath that you become aware of what each breath really means.

I spent years learning how to use my new, physically weaker body. I had to relearn how to do many of the aikido techniques I thought I knew perfectly. And finally, a few years later, I had recovered to the point that I was able to run my first marathon— with only one and a half lungs. And I never completely lost that awareness of my own breath.

Take a deep breath now: in and out. Feel what happens to your body as you breathe. Feel your shoulders rise and fall. Feel the oxygen, and the energy, moving through your body. Take just a few seconds to do nothing but breathe, and see if you don't feel just a little more clear headed.

When you exhale, your body relaxes. As you breathe in and out, you're able to see more clearly. Oxygen powers your body through everything you do.

### Give This a Try

In Chapter 1, I introduced a very basic breathing exercise to help with mindfulness. And in Chapter 5, I shared with you the STOP technique. Here is a complementary way to help you develop your own, unique *kokyu ryoku*, or breath-power:

Sitting upright and comfortable, place one hand flat on your chest and one hand flat on your belly. Close your eyes slightly—not all the way. Breathe in slowly through your nose, expanding your belly as you do so. The hand on your chest should stay still, and the hand on your stomach should feel your belly expanding outward like a balloon filling with air. Make sure your inhalation lasts for at least three seconds. Count silently to yourself: "One thousand one. One thousand two. One thousand three."

Slowly exhale through your nose, also making sure the exhalation lasts at least another three seconds. Once again, you should feel little movement with the hand flat on your chest. The hand on your stomach should feel your belly contracting. Try to pull your belly button back toward your spine.

Do this for at least five full in-and-out cycles. As you become more comfortable with the sequence, increase the in-and-out cycles to 10. You can also try to extend the three count to four and then five, and so on. Ultimately, the goal is to get to $10 \times 10 \times 10$: 10 full in-and-out cycles, inhaling for 10 seconds and exhaling for 10 seconds.

## Kokyu-Ho: Knocking Someone Over with Only a Breath

Literally, *kokyu* (pronounced, "koe-Q") means respiration. But in aikido, the concept of kokyu goes much deeper than the simple physical fact of breath. One way to translate it would be "breath-power," but even that doesn't fully do it justice. Just as your breath powers your body physically, kokyu is what powers every move you make. It generates your ki energy, which flows through all of your actions. You can't find your one-point or achieve a state of true clarity without breath-power. It's the engine that powers your entire practice of aikido. It is life.

At the beginning of every aikido class, we do an exercise called *kokyu-ho*. This is a partner exercise. You and your partner kneel in front of one another and grab each other's wrists. They'll try to push or pull you off balance while you try to stay upright and topple them over. Both of you will use your exhale—your breath-power—to power through this exercise.

It sounds simple, even silly—and that's part of the point. It's a very humbling exercise. You're going to look stupid while you're doing it. You're probably going to fall over. Your ego is going to get in the way. The more you care about not falling over, the more you're going to be tense and easily unbalanced. The more you think about how this other person is stronger or weaker than you, or how you should be better at this, the more you're going to be stuck in place, struggling to accomplish something that seems like it should be easy.

Kokyu-ho also teaches spontaneity, creativity, sensitivity, and even humility and patience. As soon as you think you're going to knock your partner over, they're going to sense your intention. You have to remain completely in the moment and find the path of least resistance, the path that allows you to change your partner's balance simply through the power of your breath. It's a physical exercise, but success relies on your mental state.

Students often fail at this exercise because they're afraid of looking silly. They hold back. They don't fully commit. Or they revert to using force to "fight" their way through the exercise. And so they fall over—and their fears are realized. How often have you done this in your life? How often have you held back because you were afraid you'd look silly, or afraid you would fall? How often have those fears made you revert to force and effort, and muscle your way through life like a bull in a china shop? And yet, in life, as in aikido, it's only when you take a deep breath and let go of your fear of losing that you can see your way to success.

## TIME TO GET UNCOMFORTABLE

Surveys have found that people rank public speaking higher on their list of fears than almost anything, including death.[1] There are deep psychological and evolutionary reasons for this fear.[2] Human beings are social animals. Alone, we're not strong enough to fight off predators. That's why we evolved to live in tribes. At some deep, instinctual level, we still feel that being part of a group is a matter of survival. And that means being laughed at, being ostracized, being rejected—these things cause a deep kind of fear that touches at the core of what makes us human. We fear public speaking because we fear this kind of social rejection. Somewhere in our deep instinctual core, we feel like failing at public speaking would be a kind of death.

Even I find it scary—still, as a professional keynote speaker, when I get out on that stage, I get nervous, and I feel myself breathing high up in my chest, the short, shallow breaths that come with anxiety and panic. In order to succeed, I have to take a minute to change my breathing. I have to center myself and breathe deeply from my belly in order to regain my calm and focus.

You don't even have to be doing a keynote speech in front of a huge crowd to feel this kind of fear. Think back to the last time you went on a job interview, or had a big, high-stakes sales call, or asked someone out on a date. Chances are good you found yourself breathing those short, shallow breaths I was talking about. It's a natural response to anxiety. But it will hold you back. In order to succeed and stay grounded during these kinds of important conversations, you need to learn to hold on to to your deep belly breathing even when you're nervous.

## ONE WAY TO GET PAST YOUR ANXIETY

So how can you practice in advance of a big presentation or an important conversation? How can you get better at using your breath-power to keep you centered when the stakes are high? There's one simple thing you can do to learn something new, overcome a common fear, and create a kokyu moment. You can do this in over 15,000 locations in 135 countries around the world: You can join your local Toastmasters club.

If you've never heard of Toastmasters, the idea is simple. There are clubs all over the world, and members usually meet weekly to work on their public speaking skills. Meetings generally last an hour, and they're designed to fit into a working person's busy schedule.

I'm a Toastmasters member myself, and I've found it immensely helpful. Each meeting offers two slots for short, prepared speeches, usually five to seven minutes. After the prepared speeches, there's a session called Table Topics. One person is assigned to come up with 10 or 15 questions, and then picks someone out of the crowd to speak on each of these topics for one to two minutes. Yes, that means that you might be suddenly summoned to the stage to speak, impromptu, for a minute or two on a topic you just heard about 10 seconds ago. The questions can be completely off the wall. Your question might be something like: *You're the cultural attaché for Scotland. You've just been invited to taste haggis for the first time. What do you do?*

> ### The Mushin Way Peak Performance Tip
> Keep your inbox uncluttered by only having 10 to 15 messages there at any one time. Studies show that by having both a clean, organized, and uncluttered physical and "electronic" workspace, such as your inbox, you are more productive, present, and stress free.

Speaking impromptu is a huge challenge. It provokes the purest form of that deep instinctual fear that makes so many people avoid public speaking at all costs. Not only are you in front of a crowd, risking your reputation and your status in the group, you're doing it without the ability to plan and prepare and make sure you're not going to say something stupid.

And that's exactly why I love it as much as I hate it. Speaking off the cuff is a perfect opportunity to practice harnessing your breath power. As soon as your name is called, you'll feel your breathing changing. You'll start breathing those shallow, panicked breaths. And you'll have to take a second to slow your breathing, focus your breath power, and get yourself centered again.

Public speaking is like any other skill—the more you practice it, the better you'll get. You'll get better and better at recognizing that moment when your breathing changes. You'll understand the meaning of that shift in your breathing, and you'll know that your nerves are natural, even instinctive. And you'll be able to deliberately shift your breathing lower in your body, slow it down, and get control of your nerves.

Once you get some practice recognizing this panic and getting it under control, you'll be able to call on this skill in a lot of different situations. So the next time you have a performance evaluation, a salary negotiation, a big sales call, or any other important conversation, you'll be able to keep yourself calm. You'll be able to harness your breath-power to stay centered during the conversation, and you'll be less likely to stumble over your words or say the wrong thing because you panic and you can't think of anything to say. Facing your fear will enable you to conquer it.

## Breathing While You Work

It's easy to acknowledge how nervousness affects you when the stakes are high. But using your breath-power is just as important in small day-to-day conversations and decisions as it is in the big moments. Breath powers everything you do. If you don't allow your breath to flow freely and bring energy to your body and your mind, you won't be able to make good decisions. You won't be operating at your full strength. You'll be like me after my lung surgery—you'll be limping along with less power than you should be able to access.

I am convinced most people don't know how to work at anything like their full potential. Most people don't organize their days to harness and enhance their power and create peak performance. Most people don't organize their days at all—and so their days unfold by chance, taking them by surprise at every turn.

If you're like most people, you spend a lot of your workday reacting, jumping from mindless task to mindless task while constantly looking at your smartphone, instead of acting. And when you're reacting, you're thrown into that shallow breath pattern. Instead of breathing deeply and pulling energy into your body deliberately, you're in a state that's not quite panic, but not quite calm—and you're in that state for most of your day. No wonder so many of us suffer from stress-related illnesses.

As I mentioned in Chapter 6, I used to be one of those people who let my day take me by surprise. I used my smartphone as an alarm clock. I'd check my work e-mail and other notifications first thing, before I was even out of bed. That meant I was starting my day in reactive mode. I would find myself doing that shallow breathing as I read e-mails alerting me to some new crisis. I'd haul myself out of bed, rush through breakfast while trying to respond to these e-mails, then hustle over to work, only to be interrupted again and again by my staff, bringing me yet more problems to attend to. I'd end up trying to squeeze my real work—the high-level strategic work that I as the CEO of the business should have been focusing on—into the cracks between crises.

Does this sound familiar? Far too many people work this way. If you don't set yourself up for success, you leave yourself exposed to anything and everything the day throws at you. You'll only get to your real work on a slow day when nothing's happening—and how many of those have you had recently?

When you pause to take a deep breath and center yourself, you can structure your day so that you have longer periods of calm in which to advance your actual work. You'll be able to harness your breath-power throughout the day and avoid those moments of shallow, panicked breathing that naturally arise when you are taken by surprise.

## How to Take Control of Your Day

Set a morning routine and stick to it. And whatever you do, don't start your day with e-mail. I don't use my phone as an alarm clock anymore. I don't look at e-mail first thing—in fact, I don't look at e-mail until much later in the day, after I've had a chance to get some real work done.

Here's how my day unfolds: I wake up to a very cool vibrating alarm clock. My smartphone is out of sight charging downstairs. When I do grab it, I don't have any push notifications on my phone showing me that I received 400 new e-mails, app messages, text messages, and the like, so there's no chance I'm going to be interrupted or thrown off by something unexpected. As a result, I'm able to have breakfast and prepare for the day in a calm and focused state.

Once I get into my office, I have a simple routine I go through before I start work. It takes about 15 minutes, and it creates an exhale moment, a moment of relaxation and calm, so that I start work in the best possible frame of mind. My grounding routine starts with a moment of prayer. Then I text one friend or family member I want to connect with—maybe I tell them hello or that I'm thinking of them. Or just send them a message to have a great day.

Then I journal, just for a minute or two, covering about half a page with whatever's on my mind—what happened yesterday, what's coming up today. Then I take a minute to read over some personal development materials—something that I've used in the past and found helpful. This routine means that I'm starting my day grounded in my connection to the universe and to my loved ones. I'm starting with a clear-eyed focus on what I'm trying to do, and a reminder of the best way I want to work.

## The Mushin Way Peak Performance Tip

Use technology—don't let it use you. You should be able to fit your entire "office" into a backpack. I use a fantastic "work" backpack by Tumi that allows me to carry my laptop, cords, files, and other odds and ends. I can work anywhere and any place I desire with my "mobile office."

After getting centered, I review my calendar items from the previous day. I move any uncompleted tasks from yesterday to today, and I organize my calendar for today. I know I'm at my most creative, productive, and present in the mornings, so I deliberately plan to give myself a couple of blocks of peak productivity time before 11:30 AM. I start with my most pressing task first, so I can approach that with a clear head and a fresh mind.

I like to work in 40-minute chunks of focused attention. I'll set a timer, work for 40 minutes, and then give myself about 5 minutes to get up, get away from my desk, and walk, preferably outside. Then I'll return to my desk and spend the remaining 15 minutes of the hour checking my e-mail or returning phone calls. Then I'll look at my calendar and see if I need to adjust my plan—did any of the messages I just received put an urgent new task on my plate? If so, I'll take a deep breath and adjust my plan.

Most people spend their days reacting. Their lives are ruled by their phones and computers and the dozens of little pings that demand attention throughout the day. That's a recipe for disaster. If you try to work this way, you'll be breathing shallowly most of the day, and you won't be using your breath-power as well as you could. But if you give yourself time to exhale, relax, and breathe deep belly breaths throughout your day, your kokyu will be working to keep you focused and help you make better decisions.

## RISKING FAILURE TO SUCCEED

Most martial arts schools earn 70 percent of their revenue from youth programs. For many people, kids in little white uniforms are the first thing they think of when they think of a martial arts class. But I had always felt my school—my academy—was different. I prided myself on teaching adults, and specifically high-achieving adults. I was an elite practitioner of a specialized craft.

The idea of teaching kids set off these negative ideas in my head, like my school was going to become a glorified daycare. Kids just didn't fit into my vision of who I was trying to be.

I believed teaching kids the discipline of aikido was impor-tant. I knew it could be incredibly valuable for a young person—martial arts had been immensely valuable to me when I studied it as a child, and aikido had become a huge part of my life since the moment I started studying it at 19. I knew the kids in my community could benefit from what I had to teach. I just didn't want to be the one to teach it to them.

Eventually, I had to face the fact that I was holding my business back. This was an easy way to essentially triple my business's income. The money I could earn from a youth program could make the school more stable, grow the business as a whole, and support my other programs. What I would teach kids would also impact their parents. I'd be introducing the concepts and benefits of aikido to adults who might eventually find themselves drawn to take classes themselves.

And why was I holding back? Because I was afraid of looking silly. I was afraid I wouldn't live up to my own inflated self-image as an elite expert. My ego had become attached to this image of myself, and I had to let it go in order to move forward. I had to exhale.

Once I accepted it was time to start trying to build a youth program, I realized I needed some help—another moment that forced me to let go of my ego. So I reached out to my network and found a martial arts school in New Jersey that had a thriving aikido youth program. I apprenticed to these folks to learn how to take this important step. Soon, I was ready to launch my own youth program. I hired staff who would help spread my vision to a younger generation.

Eventually, the youth program did triple my business's revenue and create more personal and professional opportunities than I ever could have imagined. But I could never have pulled it off unless I had been able to take a deep breath and let go of my fear—my fear that I would lose that high-powered self-image that I had been holding on to so tightly.

Starting any new venture comes with this kind of risk. For example, leaving my corporate job to start my martial arts academy in the first place required me to risk failing. Later, I had to risk failing again by letting go of the reins of my school and moving into executive coaching and consulting full time. And more than that, starting these new businesses required me to exhale and let go of certain images of myself to evolve into something new. To leave my corporate job, I had to let go of my image as a successful, well-paid businessperson. To move on from my martial arts school, I had to let go of my image of myself as a gritty entrepreneur. In both cases, I exhaled and succeeded. The risk was real, but I used it to fuel the flames of my success.

## REAL RISK, REAL REWARDS

My executive coaching client Jason was miserable at his job. He was working in the field of green architectural design, which he believed in and felt passionate about. But the corporate culture at the large company he worked for was driving him crazy. The atmosphere stifled his creativity.

And then Jason landed an opportunity to move to a smaller firm. This new company was basically a start-up. Taking this job would be risky. After all, most new companies fail—as many as 40 percent of them, according to Shikhar Ghosh, a senior lecturer at Harvard Business School.[3] Taking a job with a new company would require Jason to let go of some of his self-image as a stable, hardworking, sensible guy—but it wasn't just a risk to his ego. It was a real risk. If he did this, in a year or two he might find himself without a job. Taking this job would mean jumping into the unknown.

Still, the more Jason and I talked about this possible move, the more clearly I saw that he wanted to take this risk. He was holding on to the old job out of fear. Once he let go of that fear and put aside the ego that was attached to the generous salary he earned at his current job, it was easy to see what he had to do: He had to take the risk.

---

### The Mushin Way Peak Performance Tip

I am shocked by the amount of people who have *never* had a 60-minute massage. Turns out chronic stress is just as bad for your heart as smoking. A full-body massage lowers the levels of the stress hormone cortisol by nearly 30 percent. What are you waiting for? Go schedule your massage now— and remember to drink plenty of water afterward.

---

Jason took the job. And the company didn't fail—it was extremely successful, and Jason's star rose along with it. Even better, after taking this new job, he successfully tested for his black belt, and he met the girl of his dreams. It was like everything just fell into alignment for him. He could never have gotten to that happier, more successful place if he hadn't taken that initial risk.

Jason's fears about taking this new job weren't irrational. The company could have failed. When you leave a secure situation to try something new, you are taking a real risk. It's important to acknowledge that risk and think it through carefully. Are you at a place in your life where you're able to take that risk? Do you have a safety net that will support you if your new venture falls through? Do you have a Plan B? It's crucial to think these things through—but you won't be able to think clearly until you admit your fears and let them go. You have to separate your fear and ego from the reality of the situation in order to see whether you're willing to take that risk. And you can't do that unless you exhale. Relax. Let go for a second, and look with fresh eyes.

Don't take risks just for the sake of taking risks. And don't let fear hold you back from doing something that you want to do, that you can do, and that you are ready to do. After all, sometimes the biggest rewards come when you take real risks. And even if you take a risk and fail, you'll learn something from that failure.

## CREATING EMOTIONAL EXHALE MOMENTS

At the headquarters of NerdWallet, a personal finance company aimed at helping consumers, especially young people, make better financial decisions, there's something called a "Fail Wall." What's a "Fail Wall," you ask? Actually, it's pretty much what it sounds like: a wall in the office that's covered with notes about the staff's failures. People are encouraged to write their failures on sticky notes and put them up for everyone to see.[4] I love this idea because, as I learned during my time in the Marine Corps, Marines never retreat—we just attack from a different direction. The way I see it, a failure is nothing more than a great idea that still needs a little work. You just need to attack the idea from a different direction.

There are a couple of factors that make this wall work. First, everyone participates, including the CEO, Tim Chen. This kind of open attitude couldn't work if it didn't start at the top. Lower-level employees would be afraid to discuss their failures if they didn't see their leaders doing it. In fact, Chen is particularly up-front about his weaknesses. He has spoken openly about how he's struggled to learn to communicate effectively, and how he worries he will fail as a CEO in a way that's too big to fit on a sticky note.[5] Chen's open honesty sets the tone for the entire company to be up front about their weaknesses.

The Fail Wall also couldn't work if it were an isolated one-off. NerdWallet's management meetings start with a discussion of the team's successes and failures in the past week. The wall by itself would just be window dressing if it weren't backed up by an ongoing conversation that encourages this kind of honesty. But this company is fully committed to its culture of honesty.

The act of writing a failure down on a sticky note and putting it up where your colleagues can see it creates what I like to call emotional exhale moments. Remember, when you exhale, your body automatically relaxes. When you take a moment to breathe in deeply and breathe out, your life slows down for just a second. When you're trying to make a big decision—or even a small one—you need to find a way to let yourself relax, even if just for a moment, and slow yourself down. You need to create an emotional exhale moment.

## TRY IT YOURSELF—TODAY

You can create this kind of emotional exhale moment by doing something like what NerdWallet's staff does—openly admitting your fears and your failures. Write them down on sticky notes, if that helps. Tell them to a trusted friend, family member, or colleague. Do something to get that fear and shame out of your head, where it will prevent you from seeing your situation clearly.

Once you get those fears out of your head, you will almost certainly find they don't loom quite as large as they did when they were unspoken. This effect will be especially powerful if you're able to share your fear with someone else. After all, fears are a part of being human. And many of our deepest fears are actually the ones we all share: that we're not good enough, that we won't succeed, that people will laugh at us, that our friends and family will desert us, that we'll end up alone. Chances are, if you went to a friend and confessed that you're afraid you're no good at your job, or that you're failing as a parent, they'd say, "Me, too."

Getting these ideas out of your head and into the open can also help you do what NerdWallet's staff does thanks to its Fail Wall: Learn from your failures. If you can't admit to your failures, you can't look at them clearly, and if you can't look at them clearly, you can't learn from them. When NerdWallet's Chen writes on a sticky note that he hired an outside firm to handle the company's PR and got only five press hits in six months, that's not just a way to admit that he screwed up. It's also a way to underline the lesson learned: Nobody's going to tell the company's stories better than its own staff.

We all hold back at times because we're afraid of looking silly. Afraid of making a mistake. Afraid to fail. But there's no way to learn or grow if you don't take that risk. And even when you do fail, you will have learned something. So take a deep breath, let it out, and then move on. Make a decision. Take a risk. Learn something. And like we do in the Marine Corps, never retreat— just attack from a different direction.

## *The Mushin Way* Action Step:
## How to Apply Kokyu—Breath-Power

Psychologists Robert M. Yerkes and John D. Dodson first published an article in 1908 explaining the "comfort zone"

*(continued)*

(*continued*)

concept, which states that when you're operating from a relative level of comfort, you tend to exhibit a steady level of performance.[6] But in order to reach a level of peak performance or to truly create new and dynamic results in your life, you must step outside of that comfort zone into a slightly more stressful and anxiety-filled situation—emphasis on the word "slightly." Add too much stress and anxiety to a new situation, and performance and results plummet.

So take a deep breath and get ready to jump outside of your comfort zone in service of achieving peak performance in your life.

Challenge 1: Take up a new physical activity. For example, if you never learned how to swim or are deathly afraid of water, now is the time to learn—71 percent of the Earth is covered by water, you know. Or sign up for a martial arts class if you have never taken martial arts before. Got two left feet? Great—sign up for a dance class immediately. Afraid of heights? Take a rock-climbing class. Or join Toastmasters to get over your fear of public speaking.

The new physical activity I will do is:

_____

The start date for this new activity is:

_____

I will register and pay for this new activity by:

_____

Challenge 2: Request a 10 percent raise at work. How many excuses did you just come up with *not* to do this in the 1 second it took to read "Request a 10 percent raise at work"? Good. The resistance means there is a world of opportunity waiting for you if you can just ask your boss for a 10 percent raise. Get into action now by following the steps below:

A 10 percent raise for me is a total of $_____ per _____. (Hour, week, month, year, etc. Pick whatever works for you.) I have earned this raise because of these benefits I am currently providing my employer *above and beyond* my job description.

If you are not currently doing anything above and beyond your job description, think of three benefits you can provide your employer above and beyond your job description and start doing them immediately:

1. _____

2. _____

3. _____

Two additional benefits I can provide my employer to get this raise are:

4. _____

5. _____

I will call my boss and schedule a time to meet with him or her to discuss these five benefits I am providing to the company and request a 10 percent (or more) raise by:

_____

_____

*(continued)*

(*continued*)

Remember to let me know how it goes. Did you get the raise? More than 10 percent? Share any wins, comments, or questions with me and the entire *Mushin Way* community at michaelveltri.com/book

# CHAPTER 8

---

# 合気 *Aiki: Unity*

---

*In this chapter, you will learn why aikido teaches us never to meet force with force, but instead to blend your energy with your opponent's and use leverage to defeat even the strongest opponent. We'll discuss how to leverage weaknesses and turn them into strengths, and why you need to start by evaluating your own strengths and weaknesses with clear eyes.*

I was 16 years old and driving my parents' car when I stopped at a red light. Suddenly, I noticed a guy driving up a one-way street the wrong way, perpendicular to me. He started to inch out into the intersection and actually tapped my parents' car!

I started yelling at him. He yelled at me. Pretty soon we were both out of our cars, shouting in the middle of the street. Then he pushed me, and I pushed back.

I had been taking karate lessons for a few years. If I had remembered my karate training, I would not have let it escalate to the point of a physical fight. This guy was much bigger than me. I had no chance of winning using force against force, and winning pointless fights was not the purpose of my training anyway. But in the heat of the moment all I remembered were the karate kicks and punches I could land on this guy.

I did the stupidest thing I could have done. Just like you see in the movies, I did a supercool rear spinning back kick! Except

---

unlike the movies, instead of this guy flying backward across the street with the breath knocked out off him, he immediately caught my leg and pile-drived me into the pavement. The fight was over in a few seconds. I lost, badly. After the cops showed up and spectators pulled us apart, he came over to apologize. I was too pissed off and embarrassed to even shake his hand.

## WHAT I SHOULD HAVE KNOWN

Not that I would recommend picking a fight with some road rage idiot, but that moment was a perfect lesson in the principles that underpin aikido. That fight was force against force, and the big guy had more force behind him. Instead of thinking about what I could leverage to win against this stronger force—or, even better, considering whether it made sense to start a fight at all—I rushed in aggressively with nothing but force on my side. And I lost. I still remember how that defeat felt. And it stung all the more because it never needed to happen in the first place.

If I had known then what I know now about the principles of aikido, I would have seen the entire fight in a completely different way.

Aikido is essentially a defensive martial art. Instead of thinking about how to defeat your opponent, you think about how to blend your energy with your opponent's. This concept underpins the entire discipline. It is part of the very word *aikido*. *Ai* (合) means blending, meeting, or harmonizing, and *ki* (気) means energy; together, they mean *unifying* with your opponent, rather than dominating them.

## HARMONY IN ACTION

When you approach conflict in the spirit of *aiki*, you think about how to harmonize with the situation, so you can protect both yourself and your opponent. Instead of learning to kick and punch and strike and attack, you learn techniques to avoid and redirect your opponent's blows. You protect yourself from their attack, and you also protect your opponent by making the fight as fast and efficient as possible. You learn to leverage things in your environment, and in yourself, to overcome what is being thrown at you—instead of meeting force with force.

To succeed in the spirit of aiki (pronounced "eye-key"), you have to do two things, both of which I failed to do at that intersection when I was 16. First, you have to have the humility not to meet force with force, especially if you're facing a stronger opponent. This means clearly seeing your opponent and when necessary accepting that he is stronger. Then, you have to look for a way to use leverage instead of brute strength. This means you have to think on your feet and find ways to use your opponent's strength—or your own weakness—against them. Facing a fight this way requires self-awareness, and demands the use of your intelligence as much as your physical strength.

If I had known at 16 what I know now about how to harmonize with an attacker's energy, I could have handled the fight with a lot more dignity. I certainly would not have struck first with that ridiculous rear spinning back kick. Instead, I could have simply waited until the guy threw a punch at me—and then ducked. I could have easily avoided and then redirected his energy—to achieve aiki—instead of going unnecessarily on the attack.

Or, when he took a swing at me, I could have dropped down to one knee, hugged the guy's ankles, and leaned into his shins with my shoulder. It is simple leverage and a very basic aikido technique: If you hug an attacker's ankles so they cannot move, they will fall. It does not matter how tall they are, or how big they are, or how small you are. They will fall. Then, once he was down, I could have run away or gotten on top of the guy to hold him down until the cops came, or cooler heads prevailed. Using leverage means you do not have to be stronger than your attacker, just smarter, calmer, and more prepared.

## USING AIKI IN DAILY LIFE

I was not smart enough at 16 to approach fights this way, but I have since been able to help other young people learn how to approach the battles in their lives from a spirit of aiki. A few years ago, one of my students, Alan, came to me with a problem. His 15-year-old son, Sean, who was also a student at my dojo, was being bullied at school. And Sean was not handling it well. He had a tendency to fly into a rage when these other kids made fun of him—just like 16-year-old me in that intersection, his instinct was to try to fight force with force. And because Sean has Asperger's syndrome, his dad was having real trouble figuring out how to talk to him about these problems.

Alan and I decided to leverage Sean's knowledge of aikido to help him see the situation in a new way. The three of us sat down on some mats in the dojo, and I asked Sean what he would do if a stronger opponent came at him with an aggressive move—would he try to fight back with an aggressive counterattack?

No, of course not, Sean said. He would use one of the defensive moves that would allow him to prevail with leverage instead of brute force. He would aim for aiki, unification, instead of domination.

I explained to Sean how the bullies at school were just like a stronger opponent in an aikido bout: They want you to respond with force, because they will beat you every time. But if you instead turn, use one of your defensive moves, and look for a way to apply leverage, you will prevail.

Leveraging the language of aikido worked. Alan and I were able to connect with Sean and help him find the aiki way to deal with bullies. In the end, Sean's Asperger's—the difference that those bullies saw as a weakness—became a source of strength for him. His Asperger's gave him an incredible ability to focus. So when the name-calling and bullying began, Sean leveraged his ability to focus by deliberately taking a deep breath to calm down, disengaging from the bullies, and walking away to go join his friends. Sean is now a sophomore in college, and I expect great things from him.

## TRY IT YOURSELF

A similar technique will work wonders on bullies in the corporate world, too—the aggressive boss who tries to manage through fear, or the colleague who is always trying to push your buttons. Unfortunately, workplace bullying is all too common. A recent study by the Workplace Bullying Institute[1] found almost one in three Americans has experienced workplace bullying, and about one in five Americans has witnessed bullying in the workplace.

When a workplace bully confronts you, take a moment to think about what they want from you. They want to provoke you—to get that emotional reaction that proves that they are important and they have power over you. Do not make the mistake of fighting the force of their anger with the force of yours.

Instead, look for what you have to leverage, in both the short and long term. In the moment, stick to something simple and professional like, "I really want our project (or team, or company, or idea, or product/service, etc.) to succeed. Let me follow up with you." Use 15 words or less. This will help you restrict their ability to keep attacking you and also redirect their energy. Remember to call upon your own innate gifts, even the ones that seem like weaknesses—the sense of humor that could help you defuse a tense situation, or the sensitivity that could help you see through the bully's eyes.

In the longer term, try to build a network of friendly colleagues to leverage for support when you need it. Make sure that you're taking care of your own emotional and physical health—stress can have a serious long-term impact on your mind and body. And lay the groundwork to take concrete action if you need to. Document the incidents of abusive behavior so you're prepared to talk to your superiors if needed. If you do decide to take this type of direct action, make sure you focus the conversation on the bottom line—how the bully is making the team/company/project less productive.

Your goal in dealing with a bully should be the same as Sean's—defuse the situation in the moment, and in the longer term, focus on preserving your own health above all. Don't meet the bully where they are. Don't fight their negative energy with your own.

## USE WHAT YOU HAVE

Successful business leaders use leverage all the time. Honda was the first Japanese car company to gain a real foothold in the U.S. market. But they did not even start making cars until the 1960s, while their domestic competitors like Toyota and Nissan had been in the business since before World War II. To this day, Honda is actually one of the least-respected automobile brands in its native Japan. Honda is basically the brand you buy if you cannot afford a Toyota, or a Nissan, or a Mitsubishi, or a Subaru.

So how did they get from nowhere to the huge success of the Civic in the early '70s to the Accord in the '80s and '90s and now the CRV and other great Honda models? In the spirit of aiki, they decided to blend with the situation instead of meeting force with force. Rather than trying to overpower their bigger opponents at home, they went abroad. They leveraged the one advantage they did have: an existing manufacturing and distribution network in America, thanks to their earlier success selling lightweight motor-cycles in the U.S. market.

They also essentially leveraged their ignorance. Because they were starting from scratch when it came to consumer cars, they drew ideas from everywhere, including race cars, to create the CVCC engine that helped make the Civic both cleaner and cheaper than competing models. That allowed them to blend harmoniously with new emissions regulations that looked like huge obstacles to other manufacturers.

Honda was not stronger than their domestic competitors, but they were more creative and better at using their few small advantages to create outsize success.

## THE ROAD LESS TRAVELED

In the 1990s, I was working as a consultant in Japan, helping Western companies set up operations and tap into the Japanese market. It was not an easy job. Japan is notoriously difficult for outsiders to understand, and it tends to be a hostile market for foreign products, especially consumer products. The Japanese consumer is, quite simply, different than the Western consumer, with different tastes and priorities. As a result, many Western companies struggle to connect with them.

When Gallo Wine came to my firm for help reaching Japanese consumers, I knew we were not starting from a position of strength. At the time, Japanese people did not drink Western wine. And the country's supermarkets were part of the network of large business conglomerates known as *keiretsu* that dominated the Japanese economy at the time. These companies were tightly interwoven with each other and financially invested in one another's success. There was no way we were going to get an unfamiliar product from overseas on these supermarkets' shelves. We couldn't succeed through brute force; we needed an aiki solution.

---

### The Mushin Way Peak Performance Tip

Get a small notebook and carry it with you everywhere. I have one that actually fits in my wallet. Or ensure you have a way of easily capturing ideas with your smartphone. When an idea strikes—something to help with a current project, inspiration for a new project, something you want to say to someone in your life—write it down or capture it electronically. Review your notebook at the end of the day or the week and transfer actionable ideas to whatever productivity system you use. For ways to make all this work, check my website at michaelveltri.com/book

---

The traditional ways of doing business in Japan were not going to work in this case. So we made a virtue of our newness. Instead of trying to get inside the old, established networks, we specifically looked for people who were not a part of those networks. We hired young Japanese men in their early 20s who were a bit on the fringes of society—guys who were just a little bit quirky, a little bit nontraditional—guys who were not working for one of those big conglomerates, and did not want to. In a society where a job in a *keiretsu* was the ultimate badge of success, we leveraged these outsiders' desire to prove themselves.

We could not make connections at the top, so we made a virtue of working from the bottom of the market up. We sent these young salesmen out to make connections with little mom-and-pop stores that were not part of the big conglomerates. As a result, Gallo Wine spread through the country in a way that felt organic and natural. Instead of being imposed from some kind of central authority top-down, Gallo came into Japan in hundreds of small, unique neighborhood stores.

And it took off. The product flew off the shelves. The stores we worked with could not keep it in stock. Gallo's success started a huge red wine boom in Japan—and it never would have happened if we had not figured out how to turn the company's core weakness into a source of strength.

## START WITH SELF-AWARENESS

In America these days, most of us have been brought up to believe that we can do anything we can dream of. As an entrepreneur, I have definitely been influenced by this idea, for good or ill. It has encouraged me to pursue my dreams and push myself to succeed, but it has also led me to take on too much and wait too long to ask for help.

The principle of aiki is about unifying and blending your energy with your opponent's. In order to do this, you must start from a place of clear-eyed self-awareness. After all, if you don't assess your own energies and skills realistically, you're rushing into battle unprepared. If you believe you can do anything, if you think you are invincible, you may end up like 16-year-old me in the middle of that intersection: throwing yourself at a stronger opponent you cannot possibly defeat with force alone. It takes some humility to acknowledge that you might not be able to succeed just by trying your hardest. It takes some self-awareness to confront your weaknesses and build them into your plan for success.

So how do you get into that mind-set—the mind-set that allows you to analyze the situation and figure out, realistically, what you can and cannot accomplish?

You have to start by emptying your mind of distraction and worry. For many of us, thinking about our weaknesses can kick-start a downward spiral of anxiety. Others will too quickly jump to their own defense—"No, I do not have any experience in that field, but I'm a quick learner!" Your goal is to evaluate yourself and your resources realistically and dispassionately. And that means entering into your self-evaluation process with a clear mind.

Attaining clarity is the most important tool you have in any endeavor. Achieving true clarity can take years of practice. But you do not have to get there overnight. You can start small. For example, I take a few minutes every morning to write in a journal—it literally takes only five minutes. I just jot down a few things that are on my mind, things I am thinking or feeling, goals for the day, whatever comes to mind.

## Give This a Try

Try this yourself for a week: Set aside 5 minutes each morning to journal. Many successful people throughout history have used journaling. Ben Franklin was a prolific journal writer and took time each day to reflect on the action of the day and his goals. Mark Twain carried note-books with him when he traveled, and the observations he jotted down helped develop his witty and insightful formal writings. General George Patton kept a journal in the midst of World War II. If he can find the time to write and reflect in the middle of an invasion, you can find 5 minutes to write every morning.

There are a lot of wonderful products out there that will help you guide your writing and focus on goals for each day. There are two that I enjoy using. One is *The Five-Minute Journal*[2] because it prompts you to ask yourself what you're grateful for and what would make today great. Focusing on positive ideas like this in the morning is a great foundation for your day. And like the title says, it literally takes 5 minutes or less to use. The other one I really like is the *Fit Happens* journal.[3] It also prompts you to focus on gratitude and on simple goal setting. A simple, focused program like this will help you surface some of your strengths and weaknesses and ultimately see yourself more clearly—the first step in learning how to harmonize your energies in the aiki way.

You may also find it helpful to talk to trusted colleagues or friends about your potential blind spots—weaknesses you don't know you don't know that are holding you back from success and balance. (Think about that for a second.) Other perspectives are always useful, of course, and your friends may sometimes see things you have not, but I believe the real answers are always inside *you*. You just have to learn to quiet your mind enough that you can see them.

So talk to a few friends, and then bring their list of weaknesses or problems to one of those journaling sessions. Reflect on what others have said and run those ideas through the deepest, quietest part of your mind. Ask yourself, is this true? Is this a real problem? Will this really hold me back?

Aiki is about unifying your energy with your opponent's, rather than meeting force with force. It's about fighting smarter, not harder—assessing your own strength and your opponent's, and then determining how to proceed. Only once you have confronted your weaknesses can you start figuring out how to work around them—or turn them into strengths.

## EMBRACE YOUR WEAKNESSES

Brandi Temple of Lexington, North Carolina was not the strongest entrepreneurial fighter when she started her children's clothing business, Lolly Wolly Doodle, back in 2009. In fact, she started from a position of real weakness—her business was little more than a hobby when her husband's construction business started faltering and the family needed a new source of income. She knew almost nothing about online commerce. She had barely even used Facebook in her personal life. Yet by 2013, Lolly Wolly Doodle was an $11 million business,[4] attracting millions in venture capital funding and claiming to sell more physical products directly on Facebook than any other company in the world.

How did she do it? It started with her simply posting her handmade dresses for sale on Lolly's Facebook page and asking her fans to leave an e-mail address if they wanted to purchase one. She would then e-mail them an invoice via PayPal. A company that literally started in a garage was soon seen by investors as a potential multibillion-dollar brand.

How did she succeed where much stronger companies failed? JCPenney, for example, opened an in-Facebook online store in 2010 and closed it about a year later as a failed experiment. Other brands, including Gap, Nordstrom, and GameStop, also opened and then abandoned in-Facebook stores, finding that they weren't getting sufficient return on their investment in the experiment. Facebook commerce had been hailed as a potential $30 billion market, but most companies found that their customers wanted to keep their online shopping and socializing separate.

Temple did not try to overpower anybody. She did not attack the problem with brute force. She looked for ways to blend harmoniously with her environment. She leveraged the strengths she did have in order to create surprising success. In fact, she turned some of her weaknesses into strengths.

She was not particularly trendy or fashion-forward in her designs. Temple started out making cute but modest clothing for her own daughters to wear to church—a classic case of an entrepreneur succeeding by filling a genuine need she has experienced herself. Her customers responded to her designs precisely because they were so different from the pieces they could find in major stores. By embracing her lack of fashion savvy, she turned it into a unique strength for her brand.

### The Mushin Way Peak Performance Tip

To ensure peace of mind and to protect against theft or other electronic catastrophes, have all of your e-devices automatically and instantly backed up to the cloud (no external hard drives that can also crash, be stolen, or destroyed). Check my website for ideas on what cloud service to use: michaelveltri.com/book

She did not have a big marketing engine. She could not buy advertising to promote her brand. So she started posting her handmade dresses for sale on her Facebook page. Her lack of a marketing budget became a strength, because these offers felt like an organic part of her customers' Facebook newsfeeds, as opposed to an intrusion from a big, impersonal corporation. Essentially, she approached her customers as friends and allies instead of as targets—and as they commented on and shared her posts, they became her marketing team.

Temple also did not have much manufacturing capacity. She just had herself, her family, and some friends from church, sewing clothing in her garage. But the fact that she did not have a factory to manufacture mass quantities of dresses meant she and her team were making all their products to order, allowing them to quickly tweak their products, or make more or less of something, based on day-to-day demand. When a design sold well, she would quickly churn out a dozen variations.

Even now that the company has expanded, they are still using this same basic strategy to keep their initial outlay on a new design low and remain responsive to their market: Test small, and make a lot of something only after it has been proven to sell. What started out as the company's only option has become its best option, and its differentiating strength.

They are growing quickly now—they actually doubled their revenue several years in a row—but I would bet on Lolly Wolly Doodle and Temple to continue to succeed, precisely because they are sticking to the nimble, responsive tactics that enabled them to win from a weak position.

## ADAPT, IMPROVISE, AND OVERCOME

The Marine Corps is the smallest fighting force in the U.S. military. They also have the smallest budget. But they turn that weakness into a huge advantage. They are the few and the proud. They aim to do the most with the least resources.

So how do they do it? Discipline is important for anyone in the military, but Marines are taught to achieve their goal by any means possible. So you have to follow orders, but you also have to think for yourself and work as a team. Young Marines are given lots of responsibility, more than young recruits in other branches of the military, because at some point they will be out in the field, responsible for completing their mission no matter what happens.

Early on in our training, we learned land navigation. Your team is given this cumbersome compass, and you learn how to shoot an azimuth, or calculate an angle based off of true north, in order to make sure you are heading in exactly the right direction. There is a bit of math involved, but basically, you calculate the angle between two reference points, and a Marine goes and stands at the end of the line you are projecting (the azimuth), and then you all walk over to that Marine and you keep plotting forward from there.

Easy enough, right? Well, sure, in the middle of the day in a nice, open meadow, land navigation is fine. But when you have to do it in the dead of night in 6-foot-tall elephant grass, you literally could not see your hand in front of your face.

How would you navigate your way out of that situation?

That is what the Marine Corps teaches you. And in a different way, it is what aikido teaches, too—stay calm, stay focused, and look for something you can leverage to come up with a solution. Don't try to meet force with force. Unify your energy with your opponent's. Adapt, improvise, and overcome.

## DO YOUR OWN SELF-ASSESSMENT

Do you see your own weaknesses clearly enough to build a workable plan? When you are starting a new business or a new project, you need to be asking yourself, do I have the connections I need to get attention for this project? Do I have the social skills to sell it? Do I know enough about the market I am trying to work in? Do I have the storytelling skills to make this project compelling to potential partners and customers?

Try starting from the ideal and working your way down to the real. Look at every aspect of your project and imagine what it would look like if you were perfectly positioned to succeed. Think about your strongest competitor—what advantages do they have? Maybe, in an ideal world, you would have the elegant design of Apple and the lightning-fast turnaround times of Amazon. Maybe you would have an MBA. Maybe you would have a massively popular blog with a devoted following of commenters.

Focus on the areas where you instinctively feel like your real is farthest from your ideal. Maybe the new product you are trying to launch is not as elegant as an iPhone, but it is well designed— and your bigger weakness is slow customer service, because you do not have much manpower to throw at the problem. Or maybe you are a good enough networker, but you have always been uncomfortable promoting yourself on social media. Maybe you are okay without an MBA, but you do not know any other entrepreneurs, and your underdeveloped network is your biggest weakness.

> ### The Mushin Way Peak Performance Tip
> Here is an easy way to curb late-night snacking: Brush your teeth right after dinner! Your body and mind will get the signal that eating is over and that it's time for bed.

The idea is not to wallow in self-doubt—far from it. Ultimately, your goal is to let your examination of your weaknesses help you start brainstorming your strengths. Once you know what you cannot do, you will be able to start to see what you can do. And you'll start to see how to unify your energy with your opponent's.

One simple way to start turning your weaknesses around is to come up with a corresponding strength for each of them. Researchers from New York University recently found that associating a weakness with a positive "silver lining" improves your performance in the area of that particular strength. In other words, if you admit that you tend to be impulsive, but you tell yourself impulsive people are more creative, you will actually become more creative.

Richard Branson, the founder of Virgin Group, has done exactly this with his dyslexia. He has said that growing up, his teachers thought he was lazy because he was slow to read and complete assignments. Now he considers this weakness his greatest strength. He has come to associate his dyslexia with his ability to delegate and surround himself with the best people. He has said that he learned early to focus on doing the things he was best at, like creative thinking, and delegate the things he was not good at.

Branson is not the most humble guy in the world. But he certainly has seen the value of acknowledging his weaknesses and finding ways to work around them. And it is hard to argue with his outstanding success. What are your personal weaknesses? How could you turn them into strengths?

## FINDING A WAY

Aikido teaches its practitioners to use leverage rather than brute force. We use leverage because it is the swiftest, most compassionate, most harmonious, and most efficient way to subdue a stronger opponent and end a fight.

We have already talked about how Honda managed to leverage their motorcycle distribution network to crack the U.S. car market. But that network would never have existed in the first place if a few executives had not displayed clear-minded, dispassionate awareness in their first visit to America in 1959.

They did not start from a position of strength. There were only three of them, renting a single furnished apartment in Los Angeles. Two of them were sleeping on the floor to save money. They arrived to try to conquer a market dominated by Harley-Davidson and a couple of European manufacturers at the end of the summer—just when Americans stop thinking about buying motorcycles. They had not known the business was seasonal. In fact, they knew so little about the U.S. market that their boss, Mr. Soichiro Honda, thought that the fact that the handlebars on one of their biggest bikes kind of looked like the Buddha's moustache would be a big selling point.

They also did not know that their machines were not built to conquer America's wide-open spaces. Designed for use in Japanese cities, even their largest, most Buddha's-moustache-like machines broke down and leaked oil when driven as far and as fast as American bikers liked to drive.

It would have been easy for the three Honda execs who had been sent to LA to panic. But they kept their minds open to their surroundings. They looked at their own situation with clear eyes and a willingness to try anything. And they drove their own little, lightweight Honda motorcycles around L.A. And people started to notice them.

Those little Honda Supercubs became Honda's entry point into the U.S. market. They initially sold in retail sporting goods stores, not traditional dealerships. They sold to mainstream young people, not the traditional biker in a black leather jacket. The Supercub was not suitable for the long distances most bikers liked to ride—but that weakness actually made it much better suited to appeal to a completely new demographic. Honda aggressively marketed to this new demographic, and by 1964, about half of all motorcycles sold were Hondas—paving the way for the company's later success in the automobile market.

None of that success would have been possible if those three executives had not been able to put aside their preconceptions about how motorcycles had to be sold, along with their fears of failure, and stay open to what was happening around them. If they had clung to the idea of competing for the traditional bike-buying customer, if they had not been able to face their weaknesses and start working on creative solutions, they would not have sold any motorcycles—and Honda never would have become the American success story it is today.

### *The Mushin Way* Action Step: How to Apply Aiki—Unity

There is always a way to overcome adversity, whether on the battlefield, boardroom, or bedroom (family/personal life). In aikido, the strongest person does not necessarily win; a smaller, weaker opponent can always use leverage to achieve his or her goals—this is the essence of aiki. Many times, our strengths—think ego—can actually hold us back and prevent us from achieving our goals.

Step 1: Write down three strengths—three things you are good at doing and serve you well in your business and personal life—that may actually be holding you back from truly achieving the next level of success in your life. For example, here are three of mine:

(*continued*)

(*continued*)

1. Strong work ethic.

2. Attention to detail.

3. Committed.

Now list your three:

1. _____

2. _____

3. _____

Step 2: For the three strengths you identified, see how your ego can actually hold you back from that next big promotion or from having the most amazing personal relationship with your spouse/kids/parents. Using my example from above:

1. Strong work ethic → Not good at delegating. I take on too much and eventually burn out.

2. Attention to detail → Micromanage. I drive my employees, family, and friends nuts when I nitpick.

3. Committed → Stubborn. Sometimes I miss 10,000 other amazing opportunities because I'm so focused on THIS ONE.

Try it now:

1. _____

2. _____

3. _____

## Step 3: Aiki Insight + Relevant Action = Results

Throughout this book, I've been asking you to identify a place in your life where you are stuck—where you have been holding off making a personal or professional decision. I've been giving you simple and effective tools and techniques to help get you unstuck, into action, and producing results.

Now you have a multiplier to help you achieve results with velocity: your "Strengths as Weaknesses" list. That is, now you have a new aiki insight into where your strengths/ego are limiting your performance. Take your "Strengths as Weaknesses" list and put it somewhere where you can easily see it. Have the list on your laptop or smartphone so you are constantly reminded of where these strengths, though useful in some situations, are actually holding you back from achieving that next big promotion, raise, or harmonious home life.

I have printed and/or electronically placed my "Strengths as Weaknesses" list in these three places so I can easily see it to make sure they do not hold me back from peak performance:

1. _____

2. _____

3. _____

I have shared my "Strengths as Weaknesses" list with these three people who will tell me when they see my strengths and ego screwing things up:

*(continued)*

(*continued*)

1. _____

2. _____

3. _____

Step 4. Revisit the past exercises throughout this book and continue taking a ton of relevant aiki action—being mindful to ensure your strengths don't hold you back. And please share your progress with me and *The Mushin Way* community by posting your results, questions, and comments on my website at michaelveltri.com/book

# CHAPTER 9

# 残心 *Zanshin: Calm Awareness*

*In this chapter, you will learn how aikido principles helped me act decisively at a moment when delay would have had significant costs. You'll hear about what my aikido students have in common with spies and superheroes, and learn how an ordinary person can learn to fight off 10 attackers at once. You'll learn some simple strategies for developing your own calm awareness of a situation, and you'll see how this kind of calm awareness can help you make better decisions, leading to success and peak performance.*

On September 11, 2001, I was working at an office a few blocks from the White House. Social media and texting were both in their infancy then, so we heard about the attacks from the television one of my coworkers had on in the office. We were a small sales team—there were only six of us. When the news of the attacks broke, we all stood there for a moment, frozen in horror, watching video of the first plane flying into the tower.

I immediately knew: Our country was under attack. And my team and I were standing about a football field away from the president's house. I knew at that moment that time was of the essence. I looked around at my team and said, "Let's go!"

I led them straight down to the parking garage. We all got in our cars and drove out into the streets, which were eerily quiet. The whole city must have been glued to the television at that moment. I made it home to Georgetown in record time, still not quite sure what was happening. Cell phone networks were totally jammed with people trying to call their families, so I just sat at home watching the news unfold on TV, with the rest of the world.

That day in DC, traffic came to a standstill. Streets everywhere were blocked off by cars, trucks, and armored vehicles. Some people trying to get out of the city actually abandoned their cars and walked, for miles, to get home. It took days to clear the roads.

> ### The Mushin Way Peak Performance Tip
> See one task through to completion—don't start and stop or try to multitask. As you know, multitasking is a myth—no one can do it. Finish whatever task you start before moving on to the next one.

If my team and I had left our office even 5 minutes later, none of us would have made it home. We would have been stranded along with everyone else in the city. In that moment, my ability to see the situation clearly, with calm awareness, was the difference between my coworkers and I making it home that day or getting stuck and walking miles alongside stranded cars.

In aikido, this type of preternatural calm awareness is known as *zanshin*. Zanshin, pronounced "zahn-sheen," is a mental state when you are fully aware of everything that's happening around you. Think of a confident warrior in the middle of a battlefield or an elite NFL running back weaving through the carnage of the gridiron. They're not nervous nellies, fearfully scanning the landscape trying to figure out what's going on while they get creamed by the opposition. They are calmly aware—they just know they'll succeed, just like Master Ueshiba, the founder of aikido, was calmly aware and knew that he would avoid the bullets flying at him.

In a way, zanshin is the next step after mushin. First, you empty your mind and let go of distractions, fear, and ego (mushin). You make your mind clear like a still pond. Then you are able to enter into a state of zanshin, in which your mind reflects the situation around you like a mirror, and you're aware of any movement or change in your surroundings instantly, without needing to stop to think about it.

## REAL-LIFE DAREDEVILS

I talked a lot about zanshin when I taught aikido to a group of intelligence officers and operatives at CIA headquarters in Langley, Virginia. The group I was working with included a number of operatives training to become NOC officers—"nonofficial cover." These CIA officers are living in the murky world of *Tinker Tailor Soldier Spy* or any other John le Carré novel. They don't work out of a U.S. embassy in a foreign country. If they get caught, they do not have any backup coming to their rescue. They don't have diplomatic immunity, so getting caught means going away to a foreign prison for a long time—or disappearing forever. The stakes could not be higher when these brave men and women are out in the field serving their country.

These NOC operatives are living a double life. They can't put a toe out of line. It's absolutely crucial that they remain calm and at ease when talking to their targets, or they'll be "made" as spies. But at the same time, they have to be aware of their surroundings. The whole country around them may be hostile territory. Any individual could be a threat. They have to be ready to spring into action at a moment's notice. They have to be constantly assessing every aspect of their environment, scanning for anything unusual, searching for signs of danger.

At first glance, this seems like an impossible task: Be completely relaxed and yet completely alert. Be on your guard but totally at ease at the same time. Know where all the exits are in any room you enter—but never look for them. If we're honest, most of us would have to admit that we'd have no hope of pulling this off.

## THE SKILL THAT GIVES SPIES THEIR EDGE

So how do they do it? How do NOC officers conquer their very natural and even sensible fears and project an image of ease while remaining on high alert? Even if they don't know the word, they're practicing zanshin. They're emptying their minds of distractions and living totally in the moment. They're calmly aware of everything that's happening around them. They mark the exits in every room by feel, by instinct, without having to look, because that's how attuned they are to their surroundings.

Aikido masters, spies, and other adept practitioners of zanshin appear to have a special sense—like one of my favorite superheroes, Daredevil. In the comic book, Daredevil is blind, but his other senses are so supernaturally heightened that he possesses a kind of radar sense that works like echolocation. When you're in a state of zanshin, you can see without looking, feel without touching. It's like you've taken that sense of your own energy, or ki, that we talked about in Chapter 2, and extended it to an entire room—like proprioception that extends far beyond your own body. You know exactly where you are in space, and you know where everything else is, too. Your energy is flowing through you freely, and you're fully aware of how that energy is interacting with the energy of everything around you.

It sounds incredible. And, of course, most of us aren't blind superheroes or spies. We aren't living double lives (I hope), and we're not facing death every day. But we all do face high-stakes situations when this kind of heightened awareness would come in pretty handy. If you're negotiating a big deal with a valuable new client, you'll need to be aware of the emotional undercurrents in the room. Is the client happy with the deal? Are you pushing too hard? Do you still need to win over the key decision maker? Whose opinion really matters? The same questions need to be answered when you're interviewing for that new senior VP position—or meeting your prospective in-laws for the first time.

Zanshin can help you answer those kinds of crucial questions. And while you may never have the preternatural abilities of a master spy or a blind superhero, you can develop your ability to deepen your calm awareness of your surroundings.

## AN EXERCISE IN ZANSHIN

What would you do if 10 people attacked you at once? If you're like most people, the honest answer is probably scream for help. But I regularly teach ordinary people how to escape unscathed when facing 10 attackers.

Here's how we do it: The defender stands in the middle of a circle of 10 attackers. The attackers are all standing about 7 or 8 feet away from the defender in the middle. Sometimes these attackers have practice weapons—wooden swords or wooden staffs. Sometimes it's just 10 people about to attack you with their hands and feet—plenty threatening enough.

On the count of three, all 10 attackers strike simultaneously. They can choose to use either a downward blow (with their practice weapons or with an empty hand) or a straight thrust (with the practice weapons, or a straight jab or kick).

The defender, standing in the middle of the attacking circle, is asked to not focus exclusively on any one specific person or weapon. They should use their peripheral vision to take in the whole scene at once—practicing zanshin. When the attackers move, the defender must focus only on avoiding one incoming attacker. When that one attacker starts to move, the defender quickly "enters" (practicing irimi from Chapter 6), sliding forward in a shuffle step, their body turned slightly sideways, leading with one shoulder forward. The defender doesn't necessarily have to choose the person directly in front of them—this move will work just as well if the defender slides to the right or left.

The key is that the defender must fully commit to this action. If the defender hesitates, distracted by what's happening around them, they'll have 10 people hitting them in a millisecond. But if the defender embraces and practices zanshin and commits to entering past that one chosen attacker, then all 10 attackers will be left attacking the empty center of the circle. The defender will have quickly and confidently moved forward and past the one attacker, neatly avoiding the entire group. The circle of attackers has now collapsed in on itself, with the defender on the outside, able to flee to safety.

It's possible for anyone to escape a group of attackers this way. But if you fail to be aware, embrace zanshin, and fully commit to sliding past the one attacker, you'll get clobbered by all of them. That's why this exercise is so powerful for teaching zanshin—success depends on the ability to take in the whole scene at once and take relevant action, without getting distracted by the many things happening around you.

### Give This a Try

Try it yourself with a few friends. It can be a great team-building exercise. You don't have to use wooden swords—in fact, you probably shouldn't. Simply have one person stand in the middle surrounded by about four to six "attackers." As the attackers move forward all at once with their arms extended, the defender can then practice entering, slipping past one attacker, and turning back to face the group. You'll be surprised at how quickly you all learn how to evade your attackers.

To make it a fun team-building exercise, keep track of who successfully avoids contact with the "attackers." Whoever can perform the exercise with the least amount of contact, wins. Winner gets treated to lunch, dinner, or some other fun reward.

My aikido students and consulting clients aren't superheroes. But they can confidently do things, like successfully evade 10 attackers at once or produce an unprecedented level of business success that most people not only couldn't do but would never imagine they could do. This is what aikido teaches you: To expand your abilities and broaden your senses to make the seemingly impossible, possible.

## MOMENTS OF CALM AWARENESS

At 34 years old, I faced an impossible challenge. From the moment that I found the lump on my right testicle, I entered a bizarre new world. I was young, exercised every day, ate healthy meals—I had never really been sick a day in my life, and yet I was in danger of dying.

When I found that lump, I felt a cold shiver run down my spine. Oddly enough, I wasn't afraid. I immediately knew how I had to proceed. I didn't freak out. I didn't ignore it and hope it would go away. I made a doctor's appointment right away, and as soon as I had a diagnosis, I called my parents and let them know what was happening.

Throughout the period when I was going through my cancer treatments, I was in a state of zanshin. As I proceeded through the steps involved in my treatment—the surgery, which was at first pronounced a success; the moment six months later when I thought I'd got it beat, but my doctor told me he'd found a spot on my lung; the chemotherapy, which turned me into a zombie-like shell of myself for months; the second surgery, which left me limping along on one and a half lungs—I remained in this state of calm awareness. It was like being in the midst of a battle. I knew who and what my enemy was, and I was aware of everything I had to do to conquer it. I took one day at a time and focused on the next thing I had to do.

I was confined to a wheelchair for a while postsurgery because I was missing part of a lung and I had lost the ability to walk. My world narrowed for a while. I saw what it would be like to be elderly or disabled. I couldn't go anywhere that didn't have an elevator for me and my wheelchair. As I slowly gained strength, I began to be able to walk for short distances. I remember one day when I walked for 15 minutes, feeling great, just savoring the feeling of stretching my legs and being out in the air—and then I realized I didn't have the strength to walk the 15 minutes back! I had to sit down on a bench and call my mom to come pick me up. My progress was slow, but it was progress. And I was able to focus completely on what I had to do every day to get better.

## PREPARED FOR THE UNEXPECTED

Of course, in some ways it's easy to maintain this state of calm awareness when you're in a life-or-death situation. You're forced to focus on one thing above all else, and everything else falls away. But I also knew my previous experience and training had prepared me for my fight with cancer.

My time fighting cancer reminded me in many ways of my time in Marine Corps boot camp. For many of my fellow trainees, boot camp was an incredibly stressful time. We were all teenagers, thrown into a situation where we were getting up at 5 AM every morning, pushing our bodies to the limit, handling live grenades, shooting live weapons. You are turning yourself into a weapon of destruction—and a single wrong move could mean death for you or one of your friends. You see people around you freaking out. While I was in boot camp, two of my fellow trainees attempted suicide. They couldn't handle the pressure.

Yet for me, boot camp was one of the least stressful times in my life. I'm not any braver or stronger or tougher than the guys who didn't make it. The only difference between me and them was the deep, gut-level sense that I was doing the right thing, that I was in the right place at the right time. During boot camp, I was in perfect harmony with myself and my surroundings. That helped me achieve the clarity that I needed to find that state of calm awareness.

### The Mushin Way Peak Performance Tip

You must have a fail-safe system to capture all your inbound "stuff"—e-mails, ideas, phone calls, notes, bills, websites, reminders, lists, and so on. This way you will have peace of mind and confidence that nothing is slipping through the cracks. There are many systems to help you do this—if you don't have something in place that is working for you, I recommend you get one right away. Check my website for ideas: michaelveltri.com/book

The *esprit de corps* I felt with my fellow Marines also helped me find a deep sense of clarity and focus during boot camp. I felt something more than teamwork or camaraderie while I was there.

It was as if that feeling of being in the right place and the right time was compounded because I was also with the right team.

All of that harmony put me in the right frame of mind to develop zanshin. Boot camp was stress-free for me because I was in a state of zanshin—calmly aware of my surroundings and focused on the task at hand. And that state of zanshin was exactly what I needed to not only survive in boot camp, but thrive. To viscerally know my life was moving in the right direction and I was fulfilling my purpose.

Because I had developed the ability to move into a state of zanshin through my time in boot camp and my practice of aikido, I had that state available to me when I needed it most—when I was diagnosed with cancer. Whether or not you're facing a life-or-death situation, you will at some point in your life face a situation where the stakes are high and you need to be focused and calm. And you'll handle that situation much better if you've had some practice developing a state of zanshin.

## DEVELOPING ZANSHIN

As with any other skill, developing zanshin takes time. But it starts with something very simple that, these days, can be really difficult to find: focus.

Let's start with the easiest—and hardest—part. Your smartphone. Do you think those undercover CIA NOC operatives are out there in the field checking Facebook? You can't be aware of your surroundings when you're focused on the technological dopamine drip in your pocket. Zanshin means calm awareness, and your smartphone makes you agitated and distracted. Put it away. When you're entering into a situation where you need to be aware, turn it off and put it away where you won't be tempted to check it.

The next step is just as simple and, for some people, may be just as challenging: *Talk 25 percent less. Listen 25 percent more.* Think about this the next time you have a conversation that lasts at least a couple minutes. Anything more substantial than a quick "hi, how are you" will give you a chance to think about how much time you spend talking and how much time you spend listening. Are you dominating the conversation? Then chances are, you're not really focused on what the other person is saying. You're waiting for your turn to speak instead of really listening to what they have to say. Listening to understand is very different—and much more beneficial—than listening to respond.

When you're with someone who has this ability to truly focus, you can feel the difference. You feel validated and acknowledged. The next time you're around someone who has this ability, take some time to observe them. How do they sit or stand? What is their body language like? How exactly do you know that they're listening? How do you respond to that focused attention?

If you feel that focus is a problem for you, try to work on listening more over the next couple of weeks. Make *talk 25 percent less, listen 25 percent more* your new mantra. You'll be amazed at how much you learn about the people around you when you take the time to really listen to what they have to say. You'll find not only are you hearing more of the actual words they say, you're also noticing more about their body language, their mood, their state of mind. You'll pick up so much more information from every conversation, simply by making a small adjustment like this. And along the way, you'll develop your zanshin "muscle" more and more.

Listening is an incredibly powerful discipline because it forces you to slow down. It forces you to stay in the moment instead of letting your thoughts rush ahead to what you're going to say next. It forces you to extend your awareness beyond the inside of your own head, to take in more information from the person who's talking. When you are truly focused on listening to another person, you can move into a state that's almost meditative. It's a form of deep focus that is all too rare in our distracted modern world.

## A MOMENT OF TRUTH

I lived in Japan for 10 years. I arrived as a young Marine who was completely enamored of the country and its culture. Returning to Japan to study abroad during college and then staying there to work had given me the amazing opportunity to immerse myself in this foreign culture and learn as much as I could about it, while also learning about the corporate world. I'd found my aikido master, mentor, and lifelong friend, and I'd been challenged and enriched by my study of both aikido and Zen meditation.

During those 10 years in Japan, I accomplished much of what I'd planned to do, and I accomplished it much faster than I ever expected. I successfully tested for my black belt, became fluent in Japanese, and was extremely successful at the boutique U.S. consulting firm I worked for.

Then something happened that shocked me out of the comfortable routine I had settled into: My American boss told me he wanted to retire, and he wanted me to take over his company. It was a moment of truth—do I stay or go?

The offer to acquire the firm was tempting, of course. I was only 29 years old. Running a prestigious, highly sought-after consulting firm could have been seen as a huge step forward in my career. And I still loved living in Japan. The excitement that I'd felt when I first arrived had never really diminished. Not to mention, there were plenty of other reasons to accept this generous and flattering offer: I would be handsomely compensated while also continuing to grow and extend my professional network.

And yet I decided to turn down the opportunity and leave the country I loved so much to return to America. I am certain that turning this offer down and leaving was the right choice, and I know I couldn't have made that choice without the wisdom and focus offered by the discipline of zanshin.

---

**The Mushin Way Peak Performance Tip**

Do not use your cell phone as an alarm clock. You will start your morning distracted by the many temptations that lurk on your phone. Instead, purchase a vibrating alarm clock (*not* your cell phone set to vibrate!) for around $15. Trust me, it's one of the best investments you can make in your health and well-being.

---

Looking at this situation with calm awareness the way a warrior would survey a battlefield, I was able to see all the pros and cons of making either choice, to stay or to go. I could see why my boss wanted out—he was starting to feel trapped. All his money was in yen, and he owned real estate in Japan. Like many other expats at the time, he was stuck waiting around for the yen to bounce back. His success in Japan had become a trap. What started out as a joy for my boss—creating and growing this successful consulting firm—had now become a burden. My boss was successfully miserable.

I also knew by this point that I loved aikido and hoped to teach it someday, and a calm assessment of the situation told me there was no way I'd be able to teach aikido in Japan as a foreigner.

I loved Japan, but when I took stock of my own feelings, I realized I was starting to really miss my family and celebrating the American holidays I'd grown up with—Thanksgiving, Halloween, Christmas. I looked around at the other successful expats I knew and saw how they never fully integrated into Japanese society. I saw their kids going to college back in the States. I realized that if I stayed in Japan, I'd end up like them, with a foot in two worlds, not fully belonging anywhere. Successfully miserable.

If I took over the company and stayed in Japan, I would have fallen into the same success trap my boss was trying to escape. It would have been like staying stuck in a bad relationship. Eventually, I would have come to resent running the company and living in Japan.

## THE POWER OF ZANSHIN

Without the calm awareness to see that potential trap lurking up ahead, I might have made a huge mistake. Zanshin helped me see my situation clearly and assess all the potential opportunities and threats lurking in the dark corners. That assessment process started with mushin, with the clear mind we talked about in Chapter 5. I had to let go of my attachment to my boss's desires and my worries about what he would think. I had to let go of the ego boost I got from being the one person my boss trusted to take over his business. I had to let go of the romantic dreams that had brought me to Japan in the first place. Only by letting go of all those emotions that were clouding my judgment could I extend my attention to the whole landscape around me and see the situation clearly.

This is the power of zanshin. Without a clear mind, it's impossible to make a good decision. When your mind is full of things like guilt, ego, and fear, you're stuck inside your own head. You're not actually looking at the options in front of you—you're looking at projections of your own fear and ego. When you let go of your emotional attachment and any need to please or placate certain people, you can then clearly survey the situation around you with calm awareness. Then and only then can you see the true nature of your choice.

With zanshin, I was able to clearly see my options in their true light, as a choice between growth and stagnation, between moving on to the next phase of my life at the right time, or getting stuck in a situation that was no longer pushing me to grow in the directions I truly wanted to grow. Taking over that company would have been a temporary fix for the restlessness I was starting to feel. In the end, I chose the path that led to balance, growth, transformation, and true success.

## *The Mushin Way* Action Step: How to Apply Zanshin—Calm Awareness

Have you ever wondered why you don't accomplish your goals as fast as you'd like—if at all? You're choosing the wrong goal! The goal doesn't truly inspire you. You're choosing a goal out of guilt, obligation, fear, or just plain laziness—settling for the status quo. For example, if you hate your job and you set a goal to make more money at this dead-end job that you hate, you'll never accomplish it. No matter what.

When you practice zanshin, you are calmly aware of everything and everyone around you. You are not afraid to look into those dark corners of your mind where you know,

*(continued)*

(*continued*)

absolutely *know*, what goals truly inspire and motivate you. Zanshin shines a bright, penetrating light for you to clearly see the right path forward—the path that will allow you to transform your business and personal life to create an unprecedented level of fun and success.

Throughout this book I've been asking you to get into action and complete a decision you've been putting off making for a couple days, weeks, months, or even years. (I once put off making a decision that unnecessarily weighed on my conscience for five long years. . . .)

Here is what I want you to do:

Step 1: Review the personal and business goals you chose to work on at the end of each chapter so far. List them below:

Chapter 1 Goal:

_____

Chapter 2 Goal:

_____

Chapter 3 Goal:

_____

Chapter 4 Goal:

_____

Chapter 5 Goal:

_____

Chapter 6 Goal:

_____

Chapter 7 Goal:

_____

Chapter 8 Goal:

_____

Step 2: Cross out the ones that do not truly inspire you or that you are attempting to accomplish because you feel that you "have to," "should," or "must do."

Step 3: Are there any goals that are *not* crossed out? If so, are the remaining goal(s) inspiring enough that you will continue forward no matter what? If "no," write a new goal below that *does* truly inspire you—if it scares the heck out of you, good. That is the correct goal.

My new, inspiring goal is:

_____

_____

Now take 30 minutes to complete one action that will move your relevant and inspiring goal forward. No matter where you are or what time it is. *Do it. Now.*

Step 4: Share with me and the entire *Mushin Way* community what progress you're making, what insights and revelations you've had, or any questions and comments here: michaelveltri.com/book

# CHAPTER 10

---

# 和 *Wa: Harmony*

---

*In this chapter, you will learn why aikido emphasizes harmony and how to swiftly resolve conflict so you are not bogged down, sometimes for years, in distracting trench warfare. You'll learn some different ways harmony can help you reach peak performance and why seeking harmony doesn't mean saying "yes" to everything and everyone.*

L ess time in class, more time in recess; very little homework; parts of the school day devoted to activities like making breakfast: Finland's schools look nothing like the best schools in America. And yet the tiny Scandinavian country has become famous around the world for the consistently excellent performance of its students on an international test called the PISA Survey,[1] taken every three years by 15-year-olds from around the world.

The secret of Finland's success has nothing to do with any of the solutions currently in vogue among American educational reformers. They're not intensely prepping their kids for test after standardized test. They're not evaluating teachers based on their students' test performance. They're not—as they do in Japan—forcing kids to memorize useless facts to pass equally useless entrance exams from elementary school to college, which serve only to act as a caste categorization system for Japan's soon-to-be worker bees. Finland's students somehow manage to succeed without hiring private tutors, cramming for tests, or competing in a nationwide *Hunger Games*–style scramble to get into the country's top colleges.

## WHY THE FINNS ARE DIFFERENT

Whereas America and Japan's education systems are increasingly high-stakes, winner-takes-all competitions for scarce resources, the core value in Finland's school system is equality—*wa*. Harmony.[2] The country has no private schools. Even universities are public. All students not only start out with the same opportunities but they also leave the school system with remarkably similar outcomes. The gap between high and low achievers, as well as between rich and poor students, is small.[3] "We don't know what our kids will turn out like—we can't know if one first-grader will become a famous composer, or another a famous scientist," Krista Kiuru, the Finnish minister of education and science, told *The Atlantic*. "Everyone should have an equal chance to make the most of their skills."[4]

The Finns made a conscious choice decades ago to create a harmonious education system. Up until the 1960s, Finland separated students at age 11 into two different tracks, one more academic and one more practical. The decision to completely redesign the school system with a focus on giving all children the same education was, according to Jukka Sarjala, a former director of the country's National Board of Education, partly a moral one. The goal was balance, pure and simple. Some people worried that achievement levels would fall; instead, excellence was the byproduct of balance and harmony. Wa in action.

For children and parents struggling through the chronically underfunded, underperforming, and overstressed American and Japanese education systems, all this friendly cooperation makes

Finns sound like strange beings from another planet, not just another country. Pasi Sahlberg, the author of a recent book on Finnish schools, shares this quote from another Finnish writer: "Real winners do not compete."[5]

What? Real winners do not compete? Fierce competition is deeply ingrained in American culture and in the cultures of many other nations. To Western ears, "Real winners do not compete" may sound like *1984*-style doublespeak, like "war is peace" or "freedom is slavery." Next you'll be telling us that up is down. Black is white. What's going on here?

## FIGHTING FOR PEACE

The idea that real winners do not compete is not only at the heart of Finland's surprising educational success, but it is also at the heart of aikido as well. At a very fundamental level, the physical techniques in aikido are based on leverage, timing, and mechanics—pure physical efficiency. Why compete muscle to muscle if you are faced with an attacker who outweighs you by 100 pounds and is clearly stronger than you? There is always a more efficient way than entering into a senseless competition. At a philosophical level, aikido teaches you to tame your ego and find harmony with your fears. It's the ego that wants to scream out, "I must win no matter what!" But the flip side of that drive to win is often a fear of losing.

An aikido master would never pick a fight. In fact, not fighting and finding a better, more harmonious outcome is often the most efficient way to end a conflict. When a fight is necessary and there is no other way out of a physical altercation, of course, an aikido master would be up to the challenge. But the ultimate goal is always wa—harmony.

> **The Mushin Way Peak Performance Tip**
>
> Read the book *Quiet: The Power of Introverts in a World That Can't Stop Talking.* You will learn why and how you and others "tick" and the best way to communicate with anyone. An absolute must-read for anyone who manages people, is in a committed personal relationship, or has children.

Master Ueshiba, the founder of aikido, was a soldier, samurai, and master of many other deadly martial arts. He was also a very spiritual man who believed that peace on Earth was attainable. These two parts of his personality and background combined to create aikido. The idea is that you never have to compete with your opponent. As soon as your opponent has made the decision to attack you, he has stepped outside of harmony, and that means he has already lost.

From a Western perspective, this idea of fighting to achieve harmony instead of fighting to crush your opponent is counterintuitive. But the idea of harmony, or wa, is deeply ingrained in Japanese culture. The culture encourages solutions to problems that are good for the group or society as a whole. It discourages competition in the traditional sense. Of course, this doesn't mean passivity. Far from it. It means focusing your energy and resources in a way that creates peak performance and success without causing prolonged, distracting strife. As a Westerner living in Japan, I found much to admire in the idea and practice of wa.

In aikido, harmony is combined with grueling physical training to create a class of warriors striving for peace—"warriors of the light," as Paulo Coelho has called them.[6] An aikido master like Ueshiba would be capable of taking on any opponent, trained in any discipline, armed or unarmed. But the goal and spirit of aikido is different from most other martial arts. The Finnish idea that real winners do not compete would make perfect sense to an aikido master. In aikido, you are not so much competing as you are balancing.

Fighting to protect your opponent does not mean being unassertive. As I learned during my time in the Marine Corps, one of the most elite fighting forces in the world, securing a swift, efficient, and decisive victory is the best way to keep your opponent from harm. In fact, striving for harmony is often the secret to true, lasting victory. Think about it: Would you rather be bogged down in trench warfare for years or move swiftly toward a win-win resolution of the conflict?

### Give This a Try

You don't have to be an enlightened warrior monk like Ueshiba to start practicing harmony. Here is a very simple physical way to practice wa—harmony and balance—with your entire body. This simple act alone will increase your energy, stamina, and overall health, leading to more energy, better performance, and more creativity.

The human body is approximately 60 percent water. Yet most of us don't drink nearly enough water to ensure our body is functioning at peak performance. Water flushes toxins out of the body, regulates your internal temperature, and protects your joints, spinal cord, and other sensitive parts of your body.[7] Dehydration, even mild dehydration, can make you fatigued and cloud your mind. Studies on how much water an adult needs to drink every day have produced varying results, but the consensus is that

*(continued)*

(*continued*)

eight 8-ounce glasses of water a day is adequate for most healthy people.[8] Of course, if you exercise a lot, if you're in a hot climate, if you're sick, or if you're pregnant or breastfeeding, you'll need to drink more. But eight glasses a day is a good rule of thumb for most people, most of the time.

So now is the time to start drinking at least eight tall glasses of water per day. Track your results—either electronically with the many apps on the market, or with old-school pen and paper. One easy way to ensure you are drinking eight glasses a day is to have two glasses during breakfast, lunch, and dinner. That gets you to six. Then have one glass of water between each meal—one midway between breakfast and lunch and another glass of water in between lunch and dinner. Try it for a week and see if you don't feel better and more in balance with your body.

## HARMONIOUS HIRING

I spent many years working with Western Fortune 500 companies that were expanding into Japan, opening new offices in Asia, or beginning joint ventures with other non-Japanese companies. One of my responsibilities was as an executive recruiter, or headhunter. To successfully do business in Japan, Western firms needed to have executives with impeccable Japanese language skills and an ability to fully navigate Japanese culture. Occasionally, we'd find a Western expat whose language skills were good enough, but for the most part we needed to hire bilingual Japanese professionals. But what local successful Japanese professionals would want to take a chance on an untested new project run by a bunch of clueless Westerners?

In Japan, the corporate landscape is dominated by massive conglomerates known as *keiretsu*. Corporate culture at these firms is all-embracing. Many young, single men just starting out actually live in corporate dorms. It's like joining the military and living in a barracks. And yes—these big firms are still mostly staffed by men. Even today, in Japan women find it difficult to get hired for certain corporate jobs and, once they are hired, find the glass ceiling very, very low.

Young Japanese women go to the same elite colleges as their male counterparts. As a matter of fact, mirroring similar trends in the United States, more Japanese women than men now have college degrees.[9] They push themselves just as hard and are just as successful. Many study abroad and develop top-notch foreign language skills—primarily in English. And yet, when they graduate, they either can't find a job or they get hired for entry-level clerical positions and find they can't get promoted. Moreover, once they get married, these high-achieving females are expected to resign so they can stay at home and start raising a family.

> ### The Mushin Way Peak Performance Tip
> Never differentiate your company's product or service on price. Don't get into a price war to see which competitor can offer something for the cheapest. Sell your product or service at a premium price and make it worth it.

Surveying this landscape, I realized there was a way to win without competing. I could hire these incredibly talented, brilliant Japanese women and take advantage of this huge pool of bilingual professionals that the local Japanese companies were totally ignoring. The Western firms we were working with were thrilled to hire these highly educated bilingual women. The women were thrilled to get careers worthy of their skills. It was a win-win-win situation—even the Japanese firms that were reluctant to hire women, our potential competitors, won in the sense that they could carry on their corporate cultures without disruption.

Rather than compete head-to-head with local Japanese companies and get bogged down in trench warfare, fighting over the same pool of male worker bees they had always hired, I found a solution that allowed me to win without competing. As I was taught in the Marine Corps, I found and exploited a weak spot. As I learned in aikido, I used leverage and positioning to overcome a much stronger opponent. This is the essence of harmony—wa. The fact that I was able to advance the careers of a portion of the Japanese population that was unjustly cut off from professional opportunity was just a bonus.

This approach to the problem of hiring was perfectly in the spirit of wa, and in the spirit of aikido. And it illustrates the incredible potential of an approach to conflict that prioritizes harmony and strives to meet everyone's needs. When you aim to protect your opponent as well as yourself, you often end up seeing and seizing new opportunities that you wouldn't otherwise have seen.

## THE NEW POLAROID: WINNING THROUGH COOPERATION

Like Kodak, Polaroid was slow to respond to the digital revolution in photography. For a company known exclusively for printed photos, this could have been a fatal mistake. In fact, it almost was. Thanks in part to its failure to embrace digital photography—and in part to some legal troubles—Polaroid went through bankruptcy, twice, and churned through six CEOs in four years.[10]

Polaroid could have failed. This iconic brand could have vanished completely. It could also have attempted to compete head-to-head with the companies making the digital cameras that had nearly put it out of business. Instead, Polaroid went a completely different route: It sought out strategic partnerships.[11]

The company realized that its still-well-known brand was its biggest asset. They focused on three traits they felt defined their brand—sharing, visualization, and affordability—and went looking for companies with whom they could partner that were making products matching those traits. They licensed the Polaroid brand to companies making tablets, televisions, and a variety of small cameras designed around sharing.[12] For example, they've got a couple of small digital cameras that have built-in printers, and a small photo printer that connects to your smartphone to instantly print your Instagrams and other digital snapshots.

---

### The Mushin Way Peak Performance Tip

Every three months there is a fifth week. Depending on how the days fall, (1) March, (2) May or June, (3) August or September, and (4) November or December all have a fifth week. Start taking a few days or the entire week off to rest, recharge, do something fun and new. Eight months out of the year you only work four weeks and get by just fine. Why should these five-week months be any different?

---

Instead of competing in a market where they had no expertise and their competitors had a five- or 10-year head start, Polaroid went in a different direction. Becoming a brand-management company instead of a manufacturing company was a huge change for them. Many companies wouldn't have been able to make this kind of change. Corporations may not be people (except, oddly, in the legal sense), but they do have egos. They're run by people, after all. They can react emotionally; they can go to great lengths to avoid losing face. Polaroid had to let go of that ego in order to let go of its manufacturing business and lend out its name to other companies.

The benefits of this unexpected move were huge. Polaroid's profit margins have expanded significantly, since its overhead is so much lower. It's succeeding, and it's helping a bunch of small companies succeed in the process. The companies now making Polaroid-brand cameras would have had to struggle for years to build up the kind of brand recognition they gained instantly by partnering with Polaroid. Instead, thanks to Polaroid's decision to approach the problem in a spirit of harmony, they're now succeeding together.

Have you ever faced a situation like this in your life? Have you ever felt like you're too far behind your competition to ever catch up? Maybe you somehow got off on the wrong foot with your boss while your colleague seems to be permanently ensconced on her good side. Maybe you felt like you'd never get that goodwill back. But what if, instead of competing with this colleague, you could discover a way to practice wa and achieve true victory through harmony? When you look at a situation in the spirit of harmony and start to think about win-win situations, new opportunities often present themselves. That is the Mushin Way.

## HARMONIOUS PROGRESS

Harmony can mean cooperating with the people around you, whether they're colleagues or potential competitors—or both. But it can also mean something deeper. It can mean being in harmony with your circumstances and not trying to push or force a situation.

If you've ever tried to learn to play an instrument or speak a new language—or lose weight—you know progress doesn't come in a straight line. For many of us, this is a challenge. It's why so many guitars sit gathering dust in the backs of closets, and so many New Year's resolutions fail in February. When you can't see that you're making progress, it's hard to stay motivated.

But of course, you are making progress. It's just not happening as quickly as you want it to. I remember the frustration I felt when I was first learning aikido. I could see the beautiful movements my teachers were making—why wouldn't my body just execute those movements? I felt the same way again when I had part of my lung removed during my cancer treatments and had to relearn many of the skills I had gained over years of painstaking practice. It was like going back to being a beginner again. It was a very humbling and very frustrating experience. My fight with cancer was the same way—every time it seemed like I was getting better, I'd have another bad day.

It would be wonderful if progress happened in the way it feels like it should—a straight line, going steadily upward. It would be great if you could learn five new words in Italian every day and, at the end of a year, you'd know all the words and—hey, presto! You speak Italian. But in reality, progress comes in waves. You move forward and then you fall back. You learn a bunch of new words and then you get confused on the grammar. You lose three pounds and then you put two back on.

## Understanding How Progress Really Works

I like to picture progress as an upward sloping sine wave.[13] Remember those from math class?

A sine wave is a repetitive curve that moves up and down across an axis. Making progress in learning a new skill or advancing toward a goal is like following a sine wave along an axis that's slanting upward. Sometimes you'll be on the upswing, and sometimes you'll feel like you're sliding backward. But the overall slope of the line is upward. You will get to your goal. It just won't always feel like you're moving in the right direction.

Of course, we'd all love that curve to be as flat as possible. We'd all love to see the impact of our efforts right away. In business, if you've just gotten a promotion, started a new project, or if you're starting a new company, it's hard not to be impatient to see results—particularly if you have other stakeholders breathing down your neck. You may feel outside pressure to show results, as well as your natural internal drive to succeed. But true harmony lies in producing results over the long term and not panicking over short-term setbacks.

You must focus on staying at your one-point, nen (as discussed in Chapter 4), and not let the pressure to succeed knock you off your course. You have to be able to accept your situation for what it is—that means seeing it clearly and not focusing on a distracting tangent, but instead moving into a state of mushin where you reflect the world as it is (as discussed in Chapter 5). If you're working on bringing a new product to market and consumers aren't biting, the harmonious response is to see through your customers' eyes and take relevant action. Don't just hope it will start to sell. Harmony means seeing the situation as it is and adjusting as necessary.

Harmony means accepting things as they are, and as they are not. That means accepting with gratitude the progress we make, and also accepting with equanimity, or heiki (as discussed in Chapter 1), the setbacks we inevitably face. You will make mistakes. You will have good days and bad days. The key is not to despair on the bad days—to remember that the overall trend is upward. That as long as you keep going and don't give up, that sine wave of progress will start to pick you up again.

One way to hold onto this sense of harmony and balance is to track your progress. If you're trying to learn a language, see if you can take tests on a regular basis or join a conversation group and get people to rate your proficiency. Tracking your progress over the long term will help you look beyond day-to-day setbacks and see the overall trend.

As I explained in Chapter 8, journaling can also help you get a harmonious view of your progress. Writing down specific action steps to move your business and personal projects forward brings the sine wave to life. When you feel like you're not getting anywhere, it can be helpful to look back to a month or a year ago—how much were you struggling then? You may find you have come further than you think. Gaining this kind of perspective will help you hold to your one-point and remain in harmony with your situation.

## Tʜᴇ Hᴏɴᴏʀᴀʙʟᴇ Nᴏ

Seeking harmony means understanding the reality of your situation and accepting that situation as it is, and as it is not. It means looking for a win-win solution and finding opportunities to cooperate. It means remembering you don't have to compete to win. But it doesn't mean being passive.

In fact, in some cases the harmonious path actually involves starting a conflict. A false peace in which one or both parties is still unhappy is no real peace at all. Staying at a job you hate just because you want to avoid upsetting your boss or adding extra work to your colleagues' to-do lists is not harmonious. Approaching that situation in the spirit of wa requires you to speak up, give reasonable notice, and find a vocation that better suits you. After all, a solution isn't win-win if it's only a win for the other person and not for you.

For many of us, remembering to take responsible (not selfish) care of our own needs is the hardest part of seeking harmony. It's all too easy to spend our lives worrying about everyone else's needs first. We know our parents expect certain things of us, so we focus more on finding a "good job" than finding a job that fully uses our talents and pushes us to grow. We know our bosses are under a lot of pressure, so we take on more and more projects until we feel completely overwhelmed. We know our spouse wants to take time off to be home with the kids, so we stay on the corporate ladder even though it's not the career we dreamed of; or we'd like to take time off to watch our kids grow up, but we rush back to work in order to maintain the lifestyle we think we should have.

Mahatma Gandhi once said that "a 'no' uttered from the deepest conviction is better than a 'yes' merely uttered to please, or worse, to avoid trouble."[14] I call this "the honorable no," the no that protects you and your needs, the no that opens the way to true harmony because it respects your energies. Understanding and honoring your opponent's energies is crucial in any conflict, but you can't ignore the other side of the equation. Gandhi obviously couldn't ignore the oppression of his people just to keep a surface-level peace with Britain. True harmony had to mean freedom first.

When in your life have you needed to utter an honorable no? You may not be a freedom fighter, but you do need to build a life that protects your own ki as well as the energies of those around you. In Chapter 9, I shared the story of the time I turned down the opportunity to buy my boss's consulting company in Japan. That was an honorable no. When have you needed to start a conflict in order to seek harmony?

## The Honorable No That Saved My Company—and My Sanity

I built my aikido academy from the ground up. It took me years to make the business a success. I worked harder than I'd ever worked before. In fact, as discussed in Chapter 4, I worked way too hard, went years without taking a vacation, and completely burned myself out.

I love my aikido academy. I'm incredibly proud of it. I love my students and staff, and I'm amazed at the many lives from ages 4 to 84 that I have positively impacted over many years. But once I finally practiced what I preached and found my true one-point, I realized I was starting to hate the day-to-day management of the place. The stress of managing the business day in and day out was preventing me from being the best leader I could be. I was caught in my very own success trap, having achieved an unprecedented level of successful misery. Be careful what you wish for!

Taking some time to think about that situation helped me find the clarity to honorably say no to being successfully miserable. The more I thought about it, the more I started to think that my true calling was to bring the principles of aikido to a wider stage as a keynote speaker, author, and consultant. That's why you're holding this book in your hand.

I had to honorably say no to my very successful aikido academy in order to say yes to this higher calling. I had to honorably say no to running the day-to-day operations of my academy to create true harmony. This no wasn't what my staff wanted to hear—it meant a lot of change and upheaval, and change can make all of us anxious. But in the end, this no led to greater harmony because it respected my energies and my need to direct my energies in a new direction.

It also respected my staff's energies. Saying no and stepping back allowed my staff to step up. It gave them new opportunities to develop and grow as leaders. Ultimately, it was the right answer for everyone involved. But I had to start a conflict in order to get to that deeper state of harmony.

Where in your life right now are you saying yes merely to please or to avoid trouble? Where are you preserving a surface-level, false harmony at the expense of your own needs and ultimately everyone else's? I urge you to honorably say no and push forward to true harmony. If there's a situation in your life where you're holding onto ego and perpetuating needless conflict instead of looking for ways to cooperate, I urge you to find a way to win without competing. Make Gandhi and me proud.

Aikido teaches us that seeking peace and harmony is honorable. It also teaches us that there are different ways to achieve peace and harmony. You can't resolve a conflict by simply burying your own true thoughts, feelings, and goals any more than you can resolve a conflict by clinging to an oppositional stance and digging in to endless trench warfare. Harmony is found when all energies are in balance—yours and your opponent's.

### *The Mushin Way* Action Step: How to Apply Wa—Harmony

In their 2010 book *Well Being: The Five Essential Elements*, coauthors Tom Rath and Dr. Jim Harter gathered and conducted extensive research from 150 countries on well-being. The five broad categorizes they came up with that are most important to living a healthy and productive life are Career, Social, Financial, Physical, and Community.

Are there more well-being areas than those five broad categories? Of course. And those five broad categorizes have several subsets in them. One of my favorite well-being areas that is sometimes overlooked is known as the "third place."

After home and work, the third place is where you spend most of your time. For some people, it's church. For others it's the fitness studio or your best friends' place. Others may just love going to hear a live concert. Superman has his Fortress of Solitude. Batman has the Batcave. Everyone needs a place to retreat and recenter.

Do these environments provide you with the challenge you need physically, mentally, emotionally, spiritually? Do they allow you to de-stress, learn a new skill, or just have fun? The only way to truly transform your business and life and reach a level of effortless peak performance is to harmoniously balance all three places—home, work, and your unique third place.

*(continued)*

*(continued)*

Like Superman's Fortress of Solitude, your third place will help you rest, recharge, and renew your creative energy. Here are three simple steps to follow to create your third place:

Step 1: Write your current third place below.

My third place is:

_____

_____

Step 2: If your current third place is insufficient and uninspiring, or you don't have one yet, write three options below for a new, inspiring third place:

Three options for my new, inspiring third place are:

1. _____

2. _____

3. _____

Step 3: Take 30 minutes to get into relevant action to create your third place. No matter what time it is or where you are, *do it. Now.*

Step 4: I want to hear what unique third places you've come up with. Let me know by posting your third place ideas, comments, and questions at michaelveltri.com/book

# Conclusion
# 澄み切り Sumi-Kiri: Clarity of Mind and Body

The first time I met my aikido teacher, Professor Iwao Yamaguchi, I was lost. Literally.

It was 1990, and I was a young Marine who had just been sent to Okinawa, Japan. I'd been introduced to aikido in California and had practiced for two years, but I still didn't know much about the art. Okinawa is actually the birthplace of traditional kick-and-punch karate—aikido was a mainland Japan invention. And the Okinawans and mainland Japanese have a pretty tense relationship, dating back to atrocities committed by Japanese Imperial Army troops stationed on the Okinawa islands during World War II. So there was only one aikido school on Okinawa. And I couldn't find it.

I had an address and a phone number that a fellow Marine had given me, but that was it. I didn't speak Japanese. I didn't have a smartphone with Google Maps. The crowded streets of Okinawa were totally overwhelming to a kid from Erie, Pennsylvania. There was no way I was going to find this place on my own. So I just handed the scrap of paper with the address on it to a Japanese taxi driver and hoped for the best.

The taxi got hopelessly lost. Obviously, I was no help. So eventually, the taxi driver stopped the car, got out, and called the phone number on my scrap of paper. Two minutes later, this guy in a black-and-white martial arts uniform showed up. My future teacher had stopped in the middle of a lesson and driven his own car the very short distance to the place where the taxi driver and I had gotten stuck to come and pick me up.

Professor Yamaguchi's warm smile immediately set me at ease. He didn't speak much English, and I didn't speak any Japanese yet, but he made it clear to me that I was welcome. He brought me to his dojo, which was right above his house, and I became his student at once. It's no exaggeration to say that my life has never been the same.

## CLARITY OF MIND AND BODY

Throughout this book, I've shared amazing stories about Master Ueshiba, the founder of aikido, dodging bullets and defeating better-armed opponents through his preternatural ability of focus. That kind of total clarity of mind and body is called *sumi-kiri*, and it's the summation of everything we've talked about in this book.

The word *kiri* comes from the verb *kiru*, "to cut." Literally, sumi-kiri means "cutting through the clutter" of distractions, fear, ego, anger, and anxiety. It's the ability to find your calm energy, hold on to your one-point, achieve mushin, and understand the heart of a problem with zanshin. It's all of the concepts explained in this book, all rolled into one preternatural ability to remain calmly focused in the midst of chaos—whether in battle, the boardroom, or the bedroom (family/personal life).

When you embrace sumi-kiri, you know without knowing, see without seeing. You're aware of everything that's happening within and around you, but you're not zipping around or darting your eyes from place to place like a startled squirrel. You're alert, and not in an agitated, overcaffeinated way—you're completely calm and yet completely ready to take decisive action.

I don't think even Master Ueshiba lived in this state of full enlightenment all the time. I have achieved this state in fits and spurts. I have moments when I can feel my awareness expanding, when I know I'm fully aligned, personally, professionally, mentally, emotionally, physically, spiritually. I see this state in glimpses—and those glimpses are powerful enough to keep me striving for more of a good thing.

Achieving sumi-kiri won't erase all the problems and obstacles from your life. But when you are at or near that state of sumi-kiri, problems will become opportunities. They will cease to unsettle you. You'll be able to see that counterintuitive answer, that hidden path, that win-win solution nobody else can see. What's more, you'll be comfortable with the problems you face. You will be able to accept the world as it is and as it is not.

## THE ROAD TO ACCEPTANCE

This kind of acceptance is very difficult, even for someone like me, who has been studying aikido for many years. When you look at a situation that is not as you want it to be—a relationship that's encountering difficulties, a product that's not selling, a boss who never seems satisfied—it's hard not to want to keep tinkering around the edges of that problem. It's hard to suppress that very human impulse to deny the reality of the situation and try to "fix" the problem with a Band-Aid solution: *We just need to spend more time together. We just need a new tagline. I just need to get this big project off the ground.*

Aikido and sumi-kiri show you a different path. They show you a way to look at that problem head-on, accept it as it is, and get comfortable with the way it is not. They show you how to confront the heart of that problem and use your energies in the most direct and efficient way possible. Maybe it's having the strength to end the relationship, or going into counseling, or just having an honest conversation about what's not working. Maybe it means scrapping that product because it's just not going to work—or accepting customer criticism and redesigning the user experience. Maybe it means moving to a new department, or a new company, to get away from a toxic boss. Whatever the action is, sumi-kiri helps you see the answer clearly and find the courage to do something about it.

Master Ueshiba was a truly special individual. He was an old-school Japanese warrior in the samurai tradition. He knew how to crush his opponents when he had to. He also studied meditation for many years. In the end, he combined those two strands of his personality—the warrior and the mystic—to create this beautiful martial art. Aikido was the culmination of a lifetime of work and study.

But sumi-kiri is not something you have to wait until the end of your life to achieve. It's not something that only an extra-ordinary warrior-monk like Ueshiba can achieve. It's something to strive for, find, lose, and find again, over the course of your entire life. Starting today. Starting right now.

## LISTENING TO THE INNER VOICE

The more you practice the principles I've explained in this book, the more you'll experience this state of sumi-kiri. The closer you get to true clarity, the more you'll reap the benefits. I wouldn't suggest that you go out and try to dodge bullets or evade sword-wielding opponents, but I can promise you'll be better able to find and maintain your true path.

As you move closer to sumi-kiri, you'll find it becomes easier and easier to listen to your inner voice. In the Christian tradition, this voice is referred to as the "still, small voice," the voice of God that speaks in the silence of your heart. In Eastern traditions like Buddhism, clearing the mind and letting go of attachment and ego are believed to lead to insight and enlightenment. Personally, I like to call the insights that arise from clarity "inklings."

One of my favorite definitions of inklings comes from coachville.com:[1]

Inklings are higher intelligence: The definition of an inkling is a subtle sense of something, even with no evidence to back it up. An inkling is even quieter than intuition and even more powerful. Inklings are at the gateway of truth and as we sensitize ourselves to feel at this level, we get access to inklings and have the courage to act on them, vs waiting for them to become intuition or fact. As clients come to trust their inklings, they make better choices sooner.

An inkling is like intuition, but only the first, earliest stirrings of intuition. Like the Christian "still, small voice" or the insight that comes through meditation, an inkling develops only when your mind is still—when you've entered a state of mushin and you're working on all the principles we've discussed in this book.

The more you learn to quiet your mind, the better you'll be able to pick up the first hints of a gut feeling. Every major change I've made in my life has been the result of an inkling. When I chose to enter the Marine Corps, I did it because I had this faint intuition that it was the right course for me, and that intuition slowly grew stronger and stronger. When I decided to stay in Japan after finishing active duty in the Marine Corps, I did it because I had a gut feeling that it was the right place for me—that the next right step for me was to devote myself to studying Japanese, meditation, and aikido. And when I decided to leave Japan and return to America, I did it because I felt it was time to make a change and move on to the next phase of my life.

## CLEARING THE WAY FOR ACTION

To truly hear these subtle, life-changing whispers, you have to start to quiet your mind. Then you can hear the message in that silence. Think of it as the voice of God or the universe or your deepest self—whatever you feel comfortable with. But listen. Really try to hear what that inner voice is telling you. And then take relevant action with massive, massive support to help you succeed.

It's the relevant action that's the hard part for most of us. Maybe you have this nagging feeling you might want to go back to school—but it's just not practical, it's so expensive, you're too old, it just doesn't make sense. So you don't do it. And you keep drifting further and further from your true path. But if you're maintaining your one-point, if you have deep connections to yourself and the people around you, if you're practicing mushin and regularly emptying your mind, if you have kokyu keeping you present, you're unifying through aiki, and you have the courage to take action and enter on the center of a problem, then that little inkling of an idea will become clearer and clearer—and you'll find the courage to take relevant action. Action that leads to true victory through harmony. And a BA, or MBA, or PhD.

When you don't listen to that little voice at the center of your soul, that's when you find yourself waking up in the middle of the night, anxious and afraid. Refusing to listen to that voice causes analysis paralysis. That's what makes you sit at your desk staring at the phone, waiting as time slowly creeps by. That's what makes you ignore your potential and underperform—because you're not channeling your energy in the right direction.

When you learn to listen to that little voice and take relevant action on what you hear, you may find that you need to make a major change in your life. Or you may find that you are more fulfilled than you had let yourself believe. Only you have the answer. Only by seeking clarity will you be able to hear what that small voice is telling you.

What will your inklings tell you? Where will sumi-kiri lead you? What would your life look like if you were on your true path?

## MY TEACHER

From the day I met aikido teacher, Professor Iwao Yamaguchi, he has been a constant guiding presence in my life. I was literally lost when I met him, and even now, Professor Yamaguchi is still showing me the way. When I get the chance to talk to him or visit him in Japan, it's like a spiritual reset. He's like a bright beacon in my life, showing me the way, and every conversation with him helps me correct my course and sail on with confidence.

Yamaguchi-*Sensei* was born during World War II. Okinawa was the site of a horrific land battle, and the civilian Okinawan population was tragically abused by the Japanese imperial soldiers. There were more Okinawan civilian casualties during the war than among Japanese and American soldiers combined. During the fighting, civilians and imperial soldiers alike retreated to the caves that dotted the landscape on this volcanic island; there are tales of Japanese imperial soldiers murdering infants so that their cries wouldn't give away their position. The island was decimated by the war, and Yamaguchi-Sensei's family suffered greatly. He grew up poor, and he never went to college.

Japanese society is organized around an orderly progression from primary school to high school to college to the keiretsu. Young people push themselves to study as hard as they can, fighting at each step of the way to get into the best primary schools, the best colleges, the best companies. Everyone suffers together. Everyone ends up in pretty much the same place— toiling away in a giant corporation for the rest of their lives.

Yamaguchi-Sensei didn't do any of that. He graduated from high school and then decided to do something very un-Japanese: He became an entrepreneur. He started his own import-export company. And it was a huge success—Yamaguchi-Sensei became wealthy at a very young age. By his late 20s, he already had a fancy car, home, and all the consumer trappings. By his early 30s, he even owned his own property, an almost unheard-of accomplishment in Japan. The country has so little land that real estate is often sold with 90-year generational mortgages, on the expectation that your kids and your grandkids will inherit the property and carry on the work of paying it off. To purchase your own property as a young adult was a huge accomplishment.

And yet Yamaguchi-Sensei had the wisdom to look past all these external trappings of success and realize that he wasn't happy. He decided to sell his company and dedicate his life to the study, teaching, and dissemination of aikido. Meanwhile, his wife continued to work for one of the two major Okinawan newspaper companies. They raised four wonderful children together in a very unconventional, un-Japanese fashion.

At almost every turn, Professor Yamaguchi flouted convention. He chose to be an entrepreneur instead of going to college; he chose to devote his life to study instead of pursuing more success. He chose a wife who, unlike most Japanese women, kept working after getting married and having kids. His path kept curving in an unexpected, beautiful direction. He had the wisdom to see this, and the courage to go his own way despite all the social pressure to conform.

Even his choice of aikido as opposed to another martial art was countercultural. Karate is the traditional Okinawan martial art. Aikido was developed on the mainland, and particularly in the years after World War II, most Okinawans viewed anything from mainland Japan with suspicion. Like many young boys on Okinawa, Yamaguchi-Sensei grew up studying karate. Later, after graduating high school, he also started studying a very austere, physically demanding form of yoga. This practice started him on the path toward more spiritual practices. Eventually, he discovered aikido. Like Ueshiba, he found that this practice blended the physical and spiritual disciplines. So, despite the fact that he was an Okinawan and aikido was a mainland discipline, he opened an aikido school on Okinawa. Ultimately, that's how I found him— his was the only aikido school on the island. He was the only game in town.

## DUTY AND OBLIGATION

Yamaguchi-Sensei must have been operating from something like sumi-kiri even before he began to study aikido. Sumi-kiri cuts through the clutter of "should" and "woulds" and "coulds." It helps you see beyond the roles that have been imposed on you. It helps you see where in your life you've compromised yourself because of someone else's expectations. Did you choose your career because your parents wanted you to live up to some narrow definition of success? Do you always organize the family vacations because you're supposed to be "the responsible one"?

When you're operating from a place of sumi-kiri, you're not weighed down by guilt or obligation. You're able to cut through all those ideas about who you're supposed to be and make the right decision, the decision that protects your own essential energy, as well as the energy of those around you. After all, when you're distorting your own ki, the people around you can sense it. They'll be uncomfortable because they'll sense your discomfort. Plus, you won't be as effective as you could be, and whatever role you're playing, you'll be taking it away from someone who would be better suited for it.

Sumi-kiri helps you see your true path and gives you the courage to follow it. That's what Professor Yamaguchi has done at every step of his journey. There are many people in the world for whom that straight-line life that's so common in Japan works beautifully well. For many people, that life creates a structure in which they're able to strive to be their best selves. But that life wasn't right for Yamaguchi-Sensei, and he had the clarity to see that and, more important, the courage to find his own way.

Of course, there are many forms of duty and obligation that are honorable and encourage us to be our best selves. The sense of duty we feel as children of our parents, the obligation to help them as they age is, in many families, a beautiful and honorable thing. We all have obligations to our friends, our spouse, our children, and these obligations structure our lives in enriching ways. But the clarity of sumi-kiri helps us determine the difference between a useful duty and a sense of duty born in guilt, an obligation that does nothing but hold us back.

## STRENGTH FORGED IN PAIN

As a cancer survivor, I'm particularly drawn to stories of people who have survived tragedy or fought back against seemingly insurmountable odds. I can't think of many people who have faced greater odds with more courage than Nick Vujicic.

Vujicic was born without limbs—he has no arms or legs. Doctors couldn't find any medical explanation for his condition. It didn't seem to be a genetic disorder, and it wasn't related to damage from anything like thalidomide.[2] It seemed senseless. Doctors now know that his condition is due to something called tetra-amelia syndrome,[3] an extremely rare congenital defect that essentially just means exactly what happened to Vujicic—a child is born without limbs. Most children born this way don't live very long.[4] But Vujicic has not only survived but thrived.

Of course, it hasn't been easy. Vujicic's differences made him a target for bullies in school. He contemplated suicide when he was just 10 years old. "I felt I had no value," he has said. He eventually found hope through the idea he might be able to help someone else. "I saw a boy with no arms and legs like me, and I knew I could help him," he has said.[5]

Vujicic turned that desire to help others into a lifelong mission. He now travels all over the world, speaking to antibullying and suicide prevention groups as well as corporate audiences. His message is simple: Don't give up. "We sometimes wait for a miracle to happen in life, but the miracle never comes," he says. "I wish many things were different in my life. But knowing I can be a miracle for someone else makes my life worth living."[6]

Those words exemplify the clarity that comes from sumi-kiri. Vujicic knows better than anyone that you can't wait around for someone else to solve your problems. You can't wait for the universe to drop solutions in your lap. You have to look at your life with clear eyes, stripping away all the shame and fear that might hold you back or keep you waiting, and choose a course of action.

Aikido teaches us not to choose or prolong conflict unnecessarily. But it does not teach passivity. In fact, the clarity that comes from practicing the techniques we've discussed in this book helps move us into distinct, life-changing action. An enlightened warrior like Ueshiba wouldn't start a fight unless he had to. But he also wouldn't back down from one. And he certainly wouldn't sit around waiting for someone else to solve his problems. Sumi-kiri strips away all that's inessential and leads us to the right and honorable action. For Vujicic, that honorable action was to speak up and let others learn from his example that life is always worth living, no matter what challenges you face.

## TEMPERED STEEL

Vujicic faced unbelievable odds. My teacher, Yamaguchi-Sensei, grew up poor, his family and his people devastated by war. I wouldn't say I have suffered anything like the way these warriors have suffered, but I know I wouldn't have written this book and accomplished everything I have if I hadn't suffered through cancer. Obviously, I wouldn't wish suffering on anyone. But it's undeniable that suffering can make us stronger.

Suffering can help us cut through that clutter that obscures our true purpose. Remember, the *kiri* in *sumi-kiri* comes from the verb *kiru*, to cut. Think of those beautiful, elegant samurai swords that cut so cleanly. They're created through pressure, through fire. They're beaten and tempered, and that's what makes them so beautiful and powerful.

It's the same with us. The hard truth is that none of us gets through this life without encountering any hardship—unless we hold ourselves back and refuse to push ourselves to grow. Taking risks, failing, going through trials, all of these things help us become beautifully sharp, elegant, graceful, and powerful.

Suffering a setback, whether it's personal, physical, emotional, or professional, can be enormously clarifying. It can help us get to that state where everything inessential falls away and we see our way forward with clear eyes.

We're all wonderfully imperfect, beautifully flawed human beings. We all fail sometimes. Ultimately, that's what makes life interesting. Failure pushes us to learn something new, to grow. Hopefully, each time we suffer a setback, we gain some insight that helps us make our lives, and the lives of those around us, more abundant and joyful.

## A WORLD OF ENLIGHTENED WARRIORS

Through the clarity of sumi-kiri, we can all learn to make better decisions, to expend less of our energy fighting pointless fights and devote more of it to improving our own lives and those of everyone around us. It's a beautiful vision of a better, more useful, less stressful life. But it's even more beautiful to imagine a world full of people who see clearly and act decisively, remain centered in the midst of stress, and seek win-win solutions whenever possible.

We've talked a lot in the course of this book about the overstimulated, overstressed, always-on nature of our world today. Particularly in American culture, work is slowly but surely eating up all of our free time. We work longer and longer hours, take fewer and fewer vacations, and even when we're not technically at the office, we're expected to answer e-mails and be on call 24/7. We teach our kids to push themselves harder and harder in order to fight for a place at the best school so they can rack up tens of thousands of dollars in debt to join the same rat race that's killing us. What time we do have between crises at work, we spend distracted, connected with everyone and yet not truly connecting at all.

An enlightened warrior would never agree to live like this. When you look at our modern world through the crystal-clear lens of sumi-kiri, you can see how incredibly inefficient and badly designed our lives are. You can see, immediately and urgently, that your life has to change. You can see that you have to cut out distractions and focus on what's truly important. You can see how all of this stress and chaos is pulling you away from your one-point, and you can let go of the strings of ego and fear that keep you tied into this daily grind.

## ARE YOU READY TO TRANSFORM YOUR WORLD?

Imagine what your life could look like if you stepped away from all that day-to-day insanity and recentered your life around your true priorities. Imagine the time you'd free up by eliminating distractions. Imagine the mental energy you'd free up by letting go of the ego and fear that keep you tied to all these worn-out patterns of behavior. Imagine the creative new solutions you could come up with if you let go of your need to fight for the sake of fighting.

As you start to apply the principles you've learned in this book, you'll find your life starts to open up, to expand. You'll be less stressed and more focused. You'll make better choices. You'll have fewer enemies because you won't let your ego push you to pick unnecessary fights; instead, you'll look for ways to cooperate with or work around your opponents. You'll devote more time to what truly matters. You'll have more time for friends and family. Your life will become one of abundance, joy, and harmony. This is what allows access to effortless peak performance and balance.

And it's not just your life that will change. Your colleagues and your boss will find that work is getting done faster, with fewer pointless fights and more creative solutions. Your spouse, friends, and family will find you're more present when you're with them.

The ripple effects of the changes you're making could expand well beyond your immediate circle. What if you decide to start your own business? You could end up giving people jobs and improving the lives of multiple families. What if you come up with an innovative new product or service to help your company win without fighting? You could end up improving the lives of all of your company's customers.

Imagine a world full of people who live their lives deliberately, staying focused on their core values, seeking harmony, and acting without regard to their own fear and ego. Imagine a world full of those kinds of positive changes, rippling outward in hundreds and thousands of circles of virtue. Imagine a world full of passionate, committed, clear-eyed people like Nick Vujicic and Yamaguchi-Sensei. What would our world look like if we all freed ourselves to live our best lives? What kind of peace, balance, and abundance could we create?

I invite you to take the first step toward creating that world today. Embrace the exercises, tips, and techniques I've outlined in this book. See if you can live a more deliberate and honorable life. I promise you, you'll see positive changes immediately—and those changes will ripple outward from your life to touch the lives of others, helping to make the world a better place, one decision at a time. That's the world I want to live in—a world where we all work to make the seemingly impossible, possible. Will you join me?

# NOTES

## INTRODUCTION: THE AIKIDO WAY

1. Kisshomaru Ueshiba, *The Spirit of Aikido* (New York: Kodansha USA, 2013), 38.
2. Ibid.

## CHAPTER 1: 平気 HEIKI: EQUANIMITY

1. Sarah Rainey, "Woolwich Attack: 'I Looked Him in the Eye. I Was Sure He Wasn't Going to Kill Me,'" *The Telegraph*, May 23, 2013, http://www.telegraph.co.uk/news/uknews/terrorism-in-the-uk/10077409/Woolwich-attack-I-looked-him-in-the-eye.-I-was-sure-he-wasnt-going-to-kill-me.html.
2. Leo Hickman, "Woolwich Attack Witness Ingrid Loyau-Kennett: 'I Feel Like a Fraud,'" *The Guardian*, May 27, 2013, http://www.theguardian.com/uk/2013/may/27/woolwich-witness-ingrid-loyau-kennett.
3. Claire Duffin, "Mum Talked Down Woolwich Terrorists Who Told Her: 'We Want to Start a War in London Tonight,'" *The Telegraph*, May 22, 2013, http://www.telegraph.co.uk/news/uknews/terrorism-in-the-uk/10074881/Mum-talked-down-Woolwich-terrorists-who-told-her-We-want-to-start-a-war-in-London-tonight.html.
4. Dawn Eden, "My Catholic Faith Inspired My Actions, Says Ingrid Loyau-Kennett, Heroine Who Faced Woolwich Attacker," *Patheos* (blog), May 23, 2013, http://www.patheos.com/blogs/feastofeden/2013/05/my-catholic-faith-inspired-my-actions-says-ingrid-loyau-kennett-the-heroine-who-faced-woolwich-attacker.
5. "New Heart Sutra Translation by Thich Nhat Hanh," Plum Village, September 13, 2014, http://plumvillage.org/news/thich-nhat-hanh-new-heart-sutra-translation.

---

6. Gretchen Reynolds, "How Meditation Changes the Brain and Body," *The New York Times*, February 18, 2016, http://well .blogs.nytimes.com/2016/02/18/contemplation-therapy/?_r=0.

7. Julie Segal, "Vanguard CEO Bill McNabb Is Calm Under Fire," Institutional Investor, August 27, 2009, http://www.institutional investor.com/Article/2283026/Endowments-and-Foundations- Archive/Vanguard-CEO-Bill-McNabb-Is-Calm-Under-Fire .html?ArticleId=2283026&single=true#/.Vry9VJMrJE4.

8. Barry Ritholtz, "Vanguard's Funds Might Get Even Cheaper," *Bloomberg View*, May 15, 2015, http://www.bloombergview.com/ articles/2015-05-15/vanguard-ceo-mcnabb-s-plan-to-drive-down- costs.

9. Eric Rosenbaum, "Vanguard CEO: Expect a Lot Less from Stocks for a Decade," *CNBC*, January 25, 2016, http://www.cnbc.com/2016/01/ 25/vanguard-ceo-no-2008-but-market-will-struggle-for-gains.html.

10. Barbara Whitaker, "Besieged by Calls? Rally 'Round the Flag," *The New York Times*, September 8, 1996, http://www.nytimes.com/ 1996/09/08/business/besieged-by-calls-rally-round-the-flag.html? pagewanted=all.

11. Michael MacRae, "Red Adair to the Rescue," *The American Society of Mechanical Engineers*, December 2012, https://www.asme.org/ engineering-topics/articles/fossil-power/red-adair-to-the-rescue.

12. Maura Dolan and Lianne Hart, "Red Adair to Help Kuwait Douse Fires," *Los Angeles Times*, February 26, 1991, http://articles.latimes .com/1991-02-26/news/mn-2129_1_red-adair.

13. "Red Adair, Oil-Well Firefighter, Dies at 89," *U.S. News* at NBCNews .com, August 8, 2004, http://www.nbcnews.com/id/5641205/ns/ us_news/t/red-adair-oil-well-firefighter-dies/#.Vr49IpMrJE4.

14. Dolan and Hart, "Red Adair."

## Chapter 2: 気 Ki: Energy

1. Geoffrey A. Fowler, "Facebook: One Billion and Counting," *The Wall Street Journal*, October 4, 2012, http://www.wsj.com/articles/ SB10000872396390443635404578036164027386112.

2. Kurt Opsahl, "Facebook's Eroding Privacy Policy: A Timeline," Electronic Frontier Foundation, April 28, 2010, https://www.eff .org/deeplinks/2010/04/facebook-timeline.

3. Alexander Hotz, "Facebook Privacy: 6 Years of Controversy (Infographic)," Mashable.com, August 25, 2010, http://mashable.com/ 2010/08/25/facebook-privacy-infographic/#uoOQqFFfxgqC.

4. Hilary Lewis, "'Daily Show's' Jessica Williams on Replacing Jon Stewart: 'I'm Not Hosting,'" *The Hollywood Reporter*, February 16, 2015, http://www.hollywoodreporter.com/live-feed/jessica-williams-not-next-daily-773886.

5. Charles Clymer, "Hire Jessica Williams as the next host of The Daily Show," petition at Change.org, https://www.change.org/p/comedy-central-hire-jessica-williams-as-the-next-host-of-the-daily-show.

6. Ryan Gajewski, "Jessica Williams Is Next 'Daily Show' Host in 'Hot Tub Time Machine 2' (video)," *The Hollywood Reporter*, February 12, 2015, http://www.hollywoodreporter.com/news/jessica-williams-daily-show-host-772697.

## CHAPTER 3: 結び MUSUBI: CONNECTION

1. Kisshōmaru Ueshiba, *The Spirit of Aikidō* (New York: Kodansha USA, 2012).

2. Jeffrey Carpenter and Erick Gong, "Motivating Agents: How Much Does the Mission Matter?" Discussion Paper Series, Institute for the Study of Labor, August 2013, http://ftp.iza.org/dp7602.pdf.

3. Hans Greimel, "Why GM Struggles in Japan," *Automotive News*, August 31, 2014, http://www.autonews.com/article/20140831/ GLOBAL02/309019963/why-gm-struggles-in-japan.

4. Yoko Kubota, "Brash Image Keeps Big 3 Tiny in Japan," *The New York Times*, January 13, 2014, http://www.nytimes.com/2014/01/ 14/business/international/brash-image-keeps-big-3-tiny-in-japan .html?_r=0.

5. Lisa Vollmer, "Anne Mulcahy: The Keys to Turnaround at Xerox," Insights by Stanford Business, December 1, 2004, https://www.gsb .stanford.edu/insights/anne-mulcahy-keys-turnaround-xerox.

6. Lance Whitney, "Xerox CEO Anne Mulcahy to Retire," *CNET*, May 21, 2009, http://www.cnet.com/news/xerox-ceo-anne-mulcahy-to-retire.

7. Bill George, "America's Best Leaders: Anne Mulcahy, Xerox CEO," *U.S. News & World Report*, November 19, 2008, http://www.usnews.com/news/best-leaders/articles/2008/11/19/americas-best-leaders-anne-mulcahy-xerox-ceo.

8. Adam Bryant, "The Keeper of That Tapping Pen," *The New York Times*, March 21, 2009, http://www.nytimes.com/2009/03/22/business/22corner.html.

9. Adam Werbach, "How Xerox Tapped the Power of Reuse," *Fast Company*, July 1, 2009, http://www.fastcompany.com/1297924/how-xerox-tapped-power-reuse.

## CHAPTER 4: 念 NEN: ONE-POINT

1. Doni Bloomfield and Noah Buhayar, "Buffett Follows 'Avarice' Warning by Keeping $100,000 Salary," *Bloomberg*, March 13, 2015, http://www.bloomberg.com/news/articles/2015-03-13/buffett-follows-avarice-warning-by-sticking-to-100-000-salary.

2. Warren Buffett, letter to Berkshire Hathaway investors, February 27, 2015, http://www.berkshirehathaway.com/letters/2014ltr.pdf.

3. Susan Cain, *Quiet: The Power of Introverts in a World That Can't Stop Talking* (New York: Crown Publishers, 2012).

4. Ibid.

5. "84 Percent of Executives Have Canceled a Vacation Due to 'Demands at Work' According to Korn Ferry Survey," Korn Ferry press release, June 13, 2014, http://www.kornferry.com/press/15179.

6. Accomplishment Coaching website, http://www.accomplishment-coaching.com.

7. Bryan Burrough, "The Inside Story of the Civil War for the Soul of NBC News," *Vanity Fair*, April 7, 2015, http://www.vanityfair.com/news/2015/04/nbc-news-brian-williams-scandal-comcast.

# CHAPTER 5: 無心 MUSHIN: NO-MIND/NO-DISTRACTIONS/NO-FEAR

1. Paul Grossman et al., "Mindfulness-Based Stress Reduction and Health Benefits," *Journal of Psychosomatic Research* 57, no. 1, July 2004, 35–43.
2. David Brendell and Emmie Roe Stamell, "How Mindfulness Improves Executive Coaching," *Harvard Business Review*, January 29, 2016, https://hbr.org/2016/01/how-mindfulness-improves-executive-coaching.
3. Leigh Buchanan, "The Way I Work: Roger Berkowitz," *Inc.*, July 1, 2008, http://www.inc.com/magazine/20080701/the-way-i-work-roger-berkowitz.html.
4. Soren Gordhamer, "Bill Ford on Compassion in Business," *The Huffington Post*, February 28, 2013, http://www.huffingtonpost.com/soren-gordhamer/bill-ford-on-compassion-i_b_2781129.html.
5. "Bill Ford & Jack Kornfield," video from the Wisdom 2.0 conference, posted February 24, 2013, https://www.jackkornfield.com/bill-ford-jack-kornfield.
6. Peter Cohan, "Transcendental Meditation: Good for Oprah and Start-Ups," *Forbes*, March 26, 2014, http://www.forbes.com/sites/petercohan/2012/03/26/transcendental-meditation-good-for-oprah-and-start-ups/#5c52f77f1719.
7. Jeannine Stein, "David Lynch Loves Transcendental Meditation," *Seattle Times*, March 20, 2012, http://www.seattletimes.com/seattle-news/health/david-lynch-loves-transcendental-meditation.
8. Judy Lin, "Mindfulness Reduces Stress, Promotes Resilience," *UCLA Today*, July 29, 2009, http://newsroom.ucla.edu/stories/using-mindfulness-to-reduce-stress-96966.
9. John Tierney, "Do You Suffer from Decision Fatigue?" *The New York Times Magazine*, August 17, 2011, http://www.nytimes.com/2011/08/21/magazine/do-you-suffer-from-decision-fatigue.html?_r=0.
10. Gardiner Morse, "Decisions and Desire," *Harvard Business Review*, January 2006, https://hbr.org/2006/01/decisions-and-desire.

## Chapter 6: 入り身 Irimi: To Enter

1. Claudia H. Deutsch, "At Kodak, Some Old Things Are New Again," *The New York Times*, May 2, 2008, http://www.nytimes.com/2008/05/02/technology/02kodak.html?_r=0.
2. Chunka Mui, "How Kodak Failed," *Forbes*, January 18, 2012, http://www.forbes.com/sites/chunkamui/2012/01/18/how-kodak-failed/#10099eefbd6a.
3. Elise Hu, "New Numbers Back Up Our Obsession with Phones," All Tech Considered, National Public Radio, October 10, 2013, http://www.npr.org/sections/alltechconsidered/2013/10/09/230867952/new-numbers-back-up-our-obsession-with-phones.
4. Jennifer Deal, "Welcome to the 72-Hour Work Week," *Harvard Business Review*, September 12, 2013, https://hbr.org/2013/09/welcome-to-the-72-hour-work-we.

## Chapter 7: 呼吸 Kokyu: Breath-Power

1. Kaya Burgess, "Speaking in Public Is Worse Than Death for Most," *The Times of London*, October 30, 2013, http://www.thetimes.co.uk/tto/science/article3908129.ece.
2. Glenn Croston, "The Thing We Fear More Than Death," *Psychology Today*, November 29, 2012, https://www.psychologytoday.com/blog/the-real-story-risk/201211/the-thing-we-fear-more-death.
3. Carmen Nobel, "Why Companies Fail—and How Their Founders Can Bounce Back," *Working Knowledge* (blog), Harvard Business School, March 7, 2011, http://hbswk.hbs.edu/item/why-companies-failand-how-their-founders-can-bounce-back.
4. Jake Gibson, "Celebrating Failure: How to Make a Hit Out of Misses," *Entrepreneur*, March 19, 2014, https://www.entrepreneur.com/article/232323.
5. Maria Aspan, "The $520 Million Company That's Solving All Your Financial Needs," *Inc.*, February 2016, http://www.inc.com/magazine/201602/maria-aspan/nerdwallet-co-founder-tim-chen-on-trials-of-leadership.html.

6. Robert M. Yerkes and John D. Dodson, "The Relation of Strength of Stimulus to Rapidity of Habit-Formation," *Journal of Comparative Neurology and Psychology* 18 (1908): 459–82, http://psychclassics.yorku.ca/Yerkes/Law.

## CHAPTER 8. 合気: AIKI: UNITY

1. Workplace Bullying Institute, "2014 WBI U.S. Workplace Bullying Survey," WBI Blog, April 8, 2014, http://www.workplacebullying.org/2014-prevalence.
2. "The Five Minute Journal," Intelligent Change website, accessed September 28, 2016, https://www.intelligentchange.com?rfsn=304280.9f1aa8.
3. "Guided Journal—Fit Happens" product information page, Amazon.com, accessed September 28, 2016, https://www.amazon.com/C-R-Gibson-1003350673-Guided-Journal/dp/B00ZB5RGMO/ref=sr_1_1?ie=UTF8&qid=1475082438&sr=8–1&keywords=guided+journal+fit+happens.
4. Tom Foster, "The Startup That Conquered Facebook Sales," *Inc.*, June 2014, http://www.inc.com/magazine/201406/tom-foster/lolly-wolly-doodle-explosive-growth-from-facebook-sales.html.

## CHAPTER 10: 和 WA: HARMONY

1. Anu Partanen, "What Americans Keep Ignoring about Finland's School Success," *The Atlantic*, December 29, 2011, http://www.theatlantic.com/national/archive/2011/12/what-americans-keep-ignoring-about-finlands-school-success/250564.
2. Christine Gross-Loh, "Finnish Education Chief: 'We Created a School System Based on Equality,'" *The Atlantic*, March 17, 2014, http://www.theatlantic.com/education/archive/2014/03/finnish-education-chief-we-created-a-school-system-based-on-equality/284427.

3. Jukka Sarjala, "Equality and Cooperation: Finland's Path to Excellence," *American Educator* (Spring 2013), 32–36, http://www.aft.org/sites/default/files/periodicals/Sarjala.pdf.

4. Christine Gross-Loh, "Finnish Education Chief: 'We Created a School System Based on Equality.'"

5. Anu Partanen, "What Americans Keep Ignoring about Finland's School Success."

6. Paulo Coehlo, *Warrior of the Light: A Manual* (New York: HarperOne, 2004).

7. "Water & Nutrition," Centers for Disease Control and Prevention, last modified June 3, 2014, https://www.cdc.gov/healthywater/drinking/nutrition.

8. Mayo Clinic Staff, "Water: How Much Should You Drink Every Day?" Mayo Clinic website, September 5, 2014, http://www.mayoclinic.org/healthy-lifestyle/nutrition-and-healthy-eating/in-depth/water/art-20044256?pg=1.

9. "Japan—Country Note—Education at a Glance 2014: OECD Indicators," Organization for Economic Cooperation and Development, https://www.oecd.org/edu/Japan-EAG2014-Country-Note.pdf.

10. Dale Kurschner, "Polaroid Is Ready for Its Closeup: How the Iconic Company Is Remaking Itself for the 21st Century," *MinnPost*, April 3, 2015, https://www.minnpost.com/twin-cities-business/2015/04/polaroid-ready-its-closeup-how-iconic-company-remaking-itself-21st-cent.

11. Lisa Evans, "How Polaroid Saved Itself from Certain Death," *Fast Company*, May 15, 2014, http://www.fastcompany.com/3030562/bottom-line/how-polaroid-saved-itself-from-certain-death.

12. Alex Fitzpatrick, "Polaroid CEO: We're Now 'Curators of Innovation,'" *Time*, January 12, 2015, http://time.com/3662144/polaroid-ces.

13. Idea credit: Dino Efantis.

14. Greg McKeown, "If You Don't Prioritize Your Life, Someone Else Will," *Harvard Business Review*, June 28, 2012, https://hbr.org/2012/06/how-to-say-no-to-a-controlling.

## CONCLUSION: 澄み切り SUMI-KIRI: CLARITY OF MIND AND BODY

1. "The 15 Frameworks, Version 1.4," Coachville.com, June 13, 2002, http://www.coachville.com/15frame.html.
2. Susan Donaldson James, "'Born without Limbs' Star Inspires with Courage and 'Trust in God,'" Today.com, June 17, 2015, http://www.today.com/health/born-without-limbs-star-nick-vujicic-lives-courage-t26796.
3. Johnny Dodd, "Nick Vujicic, Born without Arms and Legs, Inspires Millions," *People*, December 4, 2014, http://www.people.com/article/Nick-Vujicic-love-without-limits-book-interview-video.
4. "Tetra-Amelia Syndrome," Genetics Home Reference, U.S. National Library of Medicine, National Institutes of Health, September 8, 2016, https://ghr.nlm.nih.gov/condition/tetra-amelia-syndrome.
5. Susan Donaldson James, "'Born without Limbs.'"
6. Ibid.

# ACKNOWLEDGMENTS

I bow deeply—*gassho*—with immense gratitude to the people who helped breathe life into *The Mushin Way* and supported, assisted, and aided in this book's creation:

First, to Nick and Sarah Moran at Public Words whose creative genius, trust, and guidance got this project off the ground, in process, and across the finish line. Without you, *The Mushin Way* would not be—thank you so much!

My literary agent Esmond Harmsworth of ZSH Literary had the insight and clarity to see the power and potential of *The Mushin Way*. Thank you, Esmond and Jane von Mehren, for your vision, guidance, and expertise in navigating the landscape of traditional publishing.

To "team Wiley": my editor, Lia Ottaviano, is one of the most knowledgeable, resourceful, and easy-to-work with people on the planet. In addition to working with Lia, I had the pleasure of working with Pete Knox and Pete Gaughan, who helped polish and refine the manuscript to a fine sheen.

I am blessed to have many friends who have provided encouragement, laughter, ideas, and a kick in the pants when I needed it. I especially want to acknowledge and thank Dino Efantis and Sean McGraw—my best friends and true brothers. I love you both very much.

Michael Callender and Tyson Geisendorff are two of my fellow black-belt brothers whom I'd be lost without. As "officers and gentlemen" having attained the rank of colonel in the U.S.

armed forces, they are inspirations to me and to everyone they come in contact with. *Semper Fi*, gentlemen. *Semper Fi!*

Gregg DeMammos and all my friends at Accomplishment Coaching—"The World's Finest Coach Training Program™"—have been instrumental in my transformation into the keynote speaker, author, and consultant I am today. You are all true "warriors of the light" and I am proud to be in your presence.

I also want to acknowledge the Ueshiba family for all their hard work and dedication in spreading aikido far and wide. I am honored to have trained with and learned from the founder's son (Kisshomaru Ueshiba), grandson (Moriteru Ueshiba), and many fine instructors and students at the Aikido World Headquarters in Tokyo, Japan. *Domo arigato gozaimashita.*

Saving the best for last, my family. My parents, Patricia and Michael Veltri, are two of the kindest, hardest working, and most loving people on the planet. It was not until I was much older that I understood the depth of their love for each other as husband and wife and the unlimited love they have for me and my two sisters, Michele and Lisa. Your love, Mom and Dad, keeps me going—it is the bright beacon that lights my way. I honor you by being a loving father and husband. I've learned from the best.

I dedicate this book to my aikido master, Professor Iwao Yamaguchi. A kind, gentle, and wise man with an unlimited capacity to live life fully present. And a wonderful, bright, and inviting smile! You are my mentor, friend, and fellow traveler on the road less traveled. Thank you for leading the way.

And finally, to all my aikido students and friends, training partners, and fellow martial artists—especially Ryan Bausch and

Noah Elliott. Thank you for your trust, patience, and for allowing me to try, fail, try again, and fail again. Until I got it right. I want you all to keep trying. Keep failing. Don't give up. You *will* get "it" right. You will succeed. Then we all get to try something new! *Kaizen*. . . .

# MICHAEL VELTRI

Visit **www.MichaelVeltri.com** to Learn More

## *Hire Michael to Speak at Your Next Event*

Michael Veltri is a top-rated keynote speaker with an exclusive system for achieving peak performance in business and life. In addition to keynote speaking, Michael is an author, consultant, and leadership expert for elite organizations such as Samsung Business, the Central Intelligence Agency, and many Fortune 500 companies.

As a professional athlete, C-suite executive, and two-time cancer survivor, Michael shares his unique message of business transformation and peak performance to audiences worldwide to:

- ☑ Achieve Rapid Results that Boost Performance and Profitability
- ☑ Attract, Retain, and Train Top Talent
- ☑ Create a Culture of Achievement and Excellence
- ☑ Increase Communication and Collaboration Between Departments and Divisions

## *Service Offerings, Benefits, and Outcomes*

### 1. *Customized Keynote Events*

- Flexible Time-Length Based on *Your Event Needs*
- Customized Content to Meet *Your Event Objectives*
- Designed and Delivered to Teach Three Unique *Mushin Way* Solution Steps Adapted to *Your Event Goals*

### 2. *Interactive Breakout Sessions*

- Engage and Interact with Michael in a Personalized Teaching Environment
- Learn, Apply, and Retain Michael's *Mushin Way* Keynote Event Solution Steps
- Q & A with Michael to Accelerate Learning

### 3. *Peak Performance Consulting Services*

- Learn Michael's Unique Consulting Tools & Techniques to Achieve Productivity, Balance, and Success;
- Effectively and Efficiently Complete Business and Personal Projects, Creating Exponential ROI;
- Enable Long-Term, Sustainable Gains Across Your Organization;

*"Michael Veltri has unlocked the mystery of peak performance."*

—JOHN OVERCAST
Director of Sales, Samsung Business

Visit **www.MichaelVeltri.com** to Learn More

# INDEX

Acceptance, in *sumi-kiri*
(clarity of mind and body),
189–190, 197–198
Adair, Red, 14–15
*Aiki* (unity), 129–150
in daily life, 132–134
developing and applying, 136,
138–139, 141, 144,
147–150
embracing weaknesses,
140–145
force-against-force *versus*,
129–130, 131–132
humility and, 131–136, 137,
140–145
leverage and, 131–137,
145–147
in the Marine Corps,
142–143
nature of, 129, 130–132,
137–140
new markets and, 134–137,
140–142, 146–147
self-awareness in, 131–136,
137–145
Aikido
described, 2
energy balance in, 2, 29–30
finding n*en* (one-point) and,
60–62

instruction in, 187–188,
193–195
life-changing action and, 198
as martial art of peace,
95–97, 171–174, 184
meditation at beginning of
class, 2
*musubi* (connection) in
teaching, 53–54
origins of, 41–42, 152–153,
172–173, 188–189, 190,
194–195
seduction of strength and,
29–31, 32–33
state of flow in, 34–35, 36–37
*zanshin* (calm awareness and),
163–164
Alarm clocks
smartphones as, 163
vibrating, 118, 163
Analysis paralysis, 86–87,
192–193
Asperger's syndrome,
132–133; 134
Authority
"command presence," 24–27
establishing personal, 93–95

Backup, automatic, 141
Berkowitz, Roger, 80